REUNITED!

Loved Ones Traced by
the BRITISH RED CROSS

The authors and publishers would like to thank
everyone who has been involved in the writing and
making of this book.

This collection of stories is taken from the files of the
British Red Cross Tracing Service, and the people and
the circumstances are real. Where necessary, names and
locations have been changed in order to protect the
identity of the people concerned, their families and the
confidential nature of the International Red Cross
Tracing Service. It is hoped that these stories, and
particularly the respect for confidentiality, will
encourage others to come forward to try and find their
families through this unique service.

The Tracing Service is a core British Red Cross
activity which is delivered at local and national level by
dedicated Red Cross staff and volunteers. The British
Red Cross works in the United Kingdom and overseas,
providing skilled and impartial care to people in need
and crisis, both personal and also when due to major
incidents. Over ninety thousand trained and skilled
volunteers, including those involved with tracing
activities, generously give their time and resources at
ninety British Red Cross Branches across England,
Northern Ireland, Scotland and Wales.

REUNITED!

Loved Ones Traced by
the BRITISH RED CROSS

Michael Johnstone

As told by
Muriel Monkhouse, O.B.E.
and Sandra Singer

AIDAN ELLIS

Details of the royalties payable to the British Red Cross can be obtained from the publisher at the following address: Cobb House, Nuffield, Henley on Thames, Oxon RG9 5RT

First published in the United Kingdom by
Aidan Ellis Publishing, Cobb House, Nuffield,
Henley on Thames, Oxon RG9 5RT

First edition 1995

A CIP catalogue record for this book is available from the British Library

Filmset by Contour Typesetters, Southall, Middx UB2 4BD
Printed in England by Biddles Ltd, Guildford,
Surrey GU1 1DA

ISBN: 0 85628 269 3

Glossary

The Red Cross Movement – the International Red Cross and Red Crescent Movement is the world's largest humanitarian organisation. It consists of more than 160 National Red Cross and Red Crescent Societies, the International Federation of Red Cross and Red Crescent Societies and the International Committee of the Red Cross. The Movement aims to protect the vulnerable and to alleviate suffering. Its work is based on seven Fundamental Principles: humanity, impartiality, neutrality, independence, voluntary service, unity and universality.

National Society – the activities of Red Cross and Red Crescent National Societies vary according to local need. Typical activities include national and international relief; health; community development; emergency response; disaster preparedness and dissemination of information.

Federation – the International Federation of Red Cross and Red Crescent Societies supports and coordinates the work of National Societies in response to natural and other disasters in non-conflict areas.

International Committee of the Red Cross (ICRC) – is an independent body, based in Geneva, whose role is to act as a neutral intermediary in humanitarian matters on behalf of people who are vulnerable and without protection, e.g. POWs, displaced civilians, etc, in situations of international conflicts, civil wars and internal disturbances. ICRC activities are mandated by International Humanitarian Law, including the Geneva Conventions.

The Central Tracing Agency (CTA) – is the part of the ICRC which coordinates international Red Cross Tracing and Message Services from and in conflict zones. It works in co-operation with the Tracing and Message sections of National Red Cross Societies and the International Tracing Service in Germany. More than sixty million records of missing people and POWs, dating from the Franco-Prussian War of 1870–71 up to the present day, are kept in Geneva.

Tracing and Message Services – under the 1949 Geneva Conventions the ICRC is mandated to re-establish contact between close family members separated by armed conflict and political upheaval. It assists in tracing separated family members and relaying family messages in crisis situations where normal postal and telecommunications have broken down. As working partners of the ICRC, National Societies are responsible for carrying out these services in their own countries.

The International Tracing Service (ITS) – was created after the Second World War in order to provide information about German and non-German civilians who had been incarcerated in concentration and forced labour camps during the war, as well as those who later became 'displaced persons'. It is based in Arolsen in Germany, financed by the German government and supervised by the ICRC.

Red Cross Delegate – delegates work for the Red Cross Movement overseas in order to fill a role that cannot be filled locally. They are highly trained and skilled professionals on salaried contracts, e.g. medical and logistics personnel.

Contents

Foreword

The International Red Cross Tracing Service
offers a lifeline of hope. It is a service which
operates under the key principles of neutrality
and impartiality and which underlines the
value of each individual human being. I have
always taken a keen interest in this service, and
have had the opportunity to see at first hand
the painstaking work undertaken by the Red
Cross both in this country and internationally.

I am sure that the personal stories reproduced
here will help others understand not only the
real value of the Tracing Service, but also the
consequences of conflict on individual human
beings, and which sometimes can take more
than a lifetime to resolve.

HRH Princess Alexandra, the Hon. Lady Ogilvy, G.C.V.O.,
Vice President of the British Red Cross

A History of Tracing

Caroline Moorehead

A Memory of Solferino, Henry Dunant's remarkable account of the battlefields during the war between Austria and France and Piedmont, in 1859, not only launched the International Red Cross Movement, but gave birth to an entirely new vision of war, what Dunant was to call 'the moral sense of the importance of human life'. For what the stocky Swiss businessman in his legendary white suit had perceived, as he walked among the wounded from the battle at Solferino, was not simply that men were dying for lack of basic medical care and even food and water, but that they felt themselves – rightly – to have been abandoned.

Survival for a soldier, in 1859, was more a question of luck than anything else. No army cared much about their own dead and severely wounded, let alone the casualties of the enemy army. Corpses were piled, unrecorded, into communal graves; the dying left to die. Who these men were, where they came from, and how their families felt, was of very little interest to anyone. 'A young Corporal named Claudius Mazuet,' wrote Dunant in his book, 'some twenty years old, with gentle expressive features, had a bullet in his left side. There was no hope for him, and of this he was fully aware. When I had helped him to drink, he thanked me, and added with tears in his eyes: "Oh, Sir, if you could write to my father to comfort my mother!" I noted his parents' address, and a moment later he had ceased to live.'

After the battle was over, Dunant went home to Geneva and soon sat down to write his memoir of Solferino, a book that was to catch the imagination of rulers and military leaders throughout the world, and lead directly to the setting up of the International Red Cross Committee in Geneva (ICRC), the Geneva Conventions and the creation of National Red Cross Societies to help wounded and sick soldiers. But he did not forget the young man who had died in his arms, traced his parents to Lyon, to number 3 Rue d'Alger, and told them what had happened to their only son. Until that moment they had known only that he was 'missing'. Without Dunant, they would never have learnt more. With this gesture came the seeds of an idea for an international tracing service, one that would provide a link between the soldier at war and his family at home, establish a point of contact and news which would lessen the dread and uncertainty experienced by people separated by war. It marked a shift from seeing soldiers not as part of an inchoate mass, but as individuals, men with names, rights and families; and it has proved one of the most crucial and successful of all the many activities of the Red Cross Movement.

Dunant was not the first person to see the need for identifying dead and wounded soldiers and establishing contact between them and their homes. In the Crimea, as in the American Civil War, some attempts had been made to help families searching for their wounded or missing relations. But in the hands of the new International Committee of the Red Cross in Geneva and its visionary founder members, the idea took shape as part of a codified attempt to bring some humanitarian concern to the brutality of war. Identifying the dead, searching for the missing, notifying families of the fate of their men at the front, and organizing an exchange of letters between prisoners of war and their relations, were all natural corollaries of the new rules of war, even if it was to be some time before they were formally enshrined in articles and conventions. 'Besides the physical pain there is moral suffering,' wrote the International Committee to the various relief committees set up during the Franco-Prussian War of 1870, 'which is no less and which we believe we could help to alleviate. We refer above all to the correspondence between the wounded fallen into enemy hands as well as unwounded prisoners, and their families.'

It was on the battlefields of the Franco-Prussian War, with the major French defeats at Sedan and Metz, when hundreds of thousands of French soldiers found themselves prisoner in Prussian fortresses and camps, that this idea acquired a more definite form. After the battle of Froeschwiller, on 4 August 1870, a large number of wounded French were taken prisoner, and lists of these men's names were soon travelling between Geneva, Berlin and Basle where a first Agency had been set up 'for information and assistance for the sick and wounded'. As it rapidly became clear that the anxiety of families who heard nothing was just as great as that of those whose men were reported wounded or dead, so the service was extended to include both the missing and the healthy. In Basle, letters and money destined for prisoners were soon pouring in at such a rate that the Agency was obliged to take over the town casino to house the hundreds of volunteers who arrived to help sort, register and despatch. From their prisons inside Prussia, the captive French soldiers themselves soon caught on to the idea, and started forwarding names that had not appeared on any list.

In October 1870, recognition in Britain of the need for direct contact between people affected by the Franco-Prussian War came with the first transfer of humanitarian messages by the British National Society for Aid to the Sick and Wounded in War, (the forerunner of the British Red Cross Society). Colonel Loyd Lindsay, who had taken money to both sides in the conflict as the Society's representative, returned from Paris with many letters for anxious relatives and colleagues waiting in England. He had insisted that these 'contain nothing likely to prove useful, or the reverse, to either besieged or besiegers'.

The Basle Agency, all agreed at the end of the war, had done much more than simply invent machinery for keeping soldiers in touch with their homes. It had provided a vital precedent. The next twenty years were to see, not so much any change of practice on the battlefields as intensive lobbying in the conference chambers. By the outbreak of the First World War, a series of resolutions had been passed at successive International Red Cross conferences, underpinned by legal agreements borrowed from both the Geneva Conventions and the Hague

Conventions of 1889 and 1907, and the International Committee had no hesitation in setting up what it called 'an international agency for assistance to and information concerning prisoners of war'. As it instructed its members, the National Red Cross Societies by now running in many parts of the world, and the different governments with which it was in touch, each belligerent state was now duty bound to set up bureaux 'to facilitate the exchange of news between prisoners and their families'.

A foolproof method for dealing with all the correspondence that now began to descend on the ICRC office in the rue de l'Athénée in Geneva was urgently needed, before the entire ICRC operation was swamped. An International Prisoner of War Agency was now officially created within the ICRC, with separate tracing departments dealing with the Central Powers and the Entente, using coloured stickers, endless forms, and a range of foreign language speakers, Serbs and Bulgarians alongside French and Swiss, working day and night, crowded into cramped offices and along narrow corridors. They had started as a handful of people. By Christmas, their numbers had grown to over a thousand. By the time of the great Belgian offensives, thirty thousand letters a day were reaching Geneva. 'You can feel the heart of Europe beating here,' wrote Stefan Zweig, the Austrian essayist and poet, after a visit to Geneva in 1917.

What made it all possible was that a system, brilliant in its simplicity, had been devised, an ordinary card index containing the name of a prisoner on one card, and that of the person being sought on another – when these two cards came

5

together and matched, the connection had been made and the family could be notified of the prisoner's whereabouts. All, of course, depended on total accuracy: when Filiol Elois could appear as Flivel Eloi or Filial Eloy, the possibility for confusion was limitless. A decision was taken to amalgamate and simplify all spellings. German names beginning with Sz, Z, Ch and Sch became one group, as did the French Lefèvres, Lefaivres and Lefebvres. With some eight to ten thousand 'Martins' on the index cards, many with the same first name and even the same regiment, every scrap of additional information became relevant. Other indexes, with dates of battles, topographical details, regimental notes, were started to provide more clues. The Agency was fast becoming a centre for information about the war itself, coming in from all directions, from the ICRC delegates mandated to visit prisoner of war camps, from charitable foundations and military sources.

No one, however, had yet had time to give much thought to civilians. But as the months passed, and it became clear that the countries at war were going to intern enemy nationals and civilians, a special department within the Agency was set up to deal with them. Its problems were almost insuperable. Unlike the military, civilians had no registration numbers. What was more, they fell, not into one simple category, but into dozens of different ones; from children stranded in occupied territories, to hostages detained without possibility of release. Worse, this was a war in which agreements had been made between some countries but not others, in which there was no unanimity of attitude from one country to another about who precisely could be labelled a political prisoner, and in which some National Red Cross Societies found themselves able to do a great deal more for detainees than others. That the Agency worked as well as it did, with over seven million cards filled in by 1918, was a testimony to the ingenuity and persistence of those who manned it.

If the ICRC was now able to look back with justifiable satisfaction on the work accomplished during the First World War, it was soon faced by challenges of another kind. The 1920s and 1930s were marked by efforts to extend the laws of war to cover civilians as well as soldiers, and to bring clarity where confusion and ad hoc arrangements had reigned. The 1930s also saw the outbreak of the Spanish Civil War. Over the question of protection of civilians, the ICRC struggled valiantly, but failed. The Second World War was to be declared before any binding agreement could be drawn up as to the fate of civilians in enemy hands. In Spain, however, it triumphed: it pioneered new ways of exchanging information and it proved beyond all doubt the value of having its own delegates in the field. Both issues were to be crucial for the Second World War.

When fighting broke out in Spain in the summer of 1936, the country was split up into two parts. In Geneva, the ICRC started a special 'Commission for Spain' and delegates hastened to Madrid and Burgos to set up agreements with both sides as to the treatment of prisoners of war. It was high summer; thousands of families were caught by the division of their country, the fathers in the cities, their families at the seaside.

7

Reunited!

The Spanish Civil War is remembered particularly for the hatreds it inspired. There was very little compassion anywhere for people taken prisoner. Summary executions became routine, while the wounded were often murdered in their hospital beds. Accurate lists of prisoners, wounded or otherwise, were impossible to come by, since the prisoners themselves were often reluctant to give their names in case of reprisals to their families, while the military on both sides refused to apply the terms of the Geneva Conventions to a civil war or to allow ICRC delegates into the prisoner of war camps. They, too, were reluctant to produce lists or names.

Bit by bit, negotiation by negotiation, using every device and stratagem they could dream up, the delegates gained concessions. Soon, exchanges between hostages from either side were being negotiated, missing children were located and returned to their families. A 'family news service', consisting of twenty-five-word messages on special cards was set up, using the system pioneered in the First World War, vastly extended and improved by consulting neighbours, friends, and even business colleagues to locate missing people. By the end of the war, five million messages had been exchanged. It was to be a dry run for what was all too soon to come.

As it turned out, the ICRC needed all the experience and imagination its staff could summon up. The Second World War was to test them as nothing had so far. Long before Hitler invaded Poland, they had created a Commission for Work in Wartime and made careful plans for a central prisoner of war agency in Geneva, vastly helped by the success of their Spanish operation, and by the new technology they were able to press into service – radios, photocopiers, telegrams, typewriters, and the electro-magnetic Watson machines, which could not only do alphabetical filing, but punch cards and sort them, print lists and copy. Even so, nothing could have prepared them for what was to come.

Repeating their excellent First World War card index system, the ICRC soon found themselves struggling to adapt to the particular demands of a war that shifted from country to country, continent to continent. When France fell, in the summer of 1940, one million and seven hundred thousand French soldiers became prisoners of the Germans; with the Italian campaign of 1943 and the Normandy landings in 1944, German soldiers, in their thousands, filled the allied prisoner of war camps. In Geneva, the tracing staff, which soon grew to over two thousand people, with branches in other Swiss cities, spent days and nights sorting, registering, forwarding and painstakingly picking through information in the hope that it would yield more clues as to the whereabouts of missing people. As more and more civilians lost their freedom in enemy occupied territory, so they did their best to open new lines of communication, endlessly thwarted by the intransigence and brutality of the occupying German forces towards civilians, and the fact that the Russians were not signatory to the 1929 Convention regarding prisoners of war, which the Germans, therefore, said did not apply. Once again, the express service message, for those without news of a soldier at the front for more than three months, and the family message, pioneered in Spain, were started up. By the end of the war, twenty million of these messages –

twenty thousand a day in the final months – had flowed throughout Occupied Europe, North Africa, Asia and the whole American continent.

The ICRC's task was made slightly lighter by the fact that National Information Bureaux had been started up by various governments at war. In Britain, as early as May 1940, the British Red Cross opened a Foreign Relations Department to deal with the growing number of people anxious for news of relations trapped in Occupied Europe; in a single week, after the fall of France, thirty thousand enquiries were made. The Foreign Relations Department did more than simply attempt to match enquirer with received information: when news came back that the address had disappeared in the bombing, or the person sought was not to be found, they launched intricate systems to trace the missing. Detective work, slow, laborious, sometimes excitingly rewarding, sometimes heart rending, absorbed the time and energy of thousands of tracers, as the opening of new fronts brought whole new nations into the war, and continued bombing turned civilians into refugees. Something of the craftiness and ingenuity of tracing and communication work can be seen from one of the ICRC's more elaborate networks. When the Germans occupied Italy, and contact needed to be made with Italians behind German lines, the ICRC arranged for mail and messages to be sent by enquirers to Geneva, then put on trucks for Marseille. There, they were transferred on to an ICRC ship bound for Lisbon, then flown in allied military aircraft to Algiers, and finally forwarded to the ICRC delegate for distribution through southern Italy.

Nothing, however, could have prepared the tracers for the chaos of post-war Europe. Forty million people had been dispersed by the war. In 1945, they were desperate for news, frantic to know what had happened to those imprisoned and interned during the course of the war, and to learn who had managed to survive. All over Europe, people driven from their homes by bombing, by the creation of new borders, by hunger, were on the move. One in every six Germans was said to have left their home and joined the fourteen to fifteen million civilians fleeing before the Red Army or expelled from territories east of the Oder-Neise. The tracers, submerged by requests and enquiries, struggled not to vanish beneath cards that grew in thousands every day. No previous war had dispersed so many people.

In Britain, there had been a meeting, early in 1943, between the Army and the Foreign Relations Department of the British Red Cross, to discuss the problems that might arise with displaced people after the allied landings in Italy. A first bureau in southern Italy, staffed by specialist tracers sent out from London, proved so efficient that as British Red Cross Commissions followed the advance of the allied troops making their way up Italy and into liberated Europe, trained tracers went with them, opening new offices as they went.

Supreme Headquarters of the Allied Expeditionary Forces, who had been given the responsibility of registering displaced civilians in the areas they liberated, asked the British Red Cross to set up tracing bureaux in the British Zone in Germany, while all over Europe other tracing offices now opened, run by other Red Cross Societies, voluntary

11

and church groups and charities, helping each other, and in constant touch with the ICRC. Day by day, week by week, families began to find each other. Many, of course, found no one. Parents, brothers and sisters, children, all lost in the concentration camps, on the Russian front, in the western desert or simply under the bombs.

War had broken out in 1939 before there had been time for anything but a draft international agreement, the Tokyo draft, on safeguarding civilians. This was to prove virtually impotent in occupied Europe and the Far East. Whereas prisoners of war were covered by a series of carefully worked out articles, civilians were vulnerable to every abuse. In Nazi-occupied Europe, no messages had reached the inmates of the concentration camps, and no lists of names of those deported and imprisoned had ever been issued. As, one by one, the concentration camps were liberated, the allied military authorities began to register survivors, as well as to commence the task of gathering documents concerning millions of forced labourers imported into Germany from the occupied countries. From graves, from information gathered from survivors, from military records and hospital registers, they also began to list the dead. It was a very slow job. Much of this work fell to the United Nations Relief and Rehabilitation Administration (UNRRA), which had been set up in Washington in 1943 by President Roosevelt and which had asked the ICRC to operate a Central Tracing Agency. Early in 1946, this agency moved to new headquarters in Arolsen, a small town in Hesse in central Germany, chosen for its position at the heart of the four occupation zones, and because the town contained several very large, undamaged buildings suitable for storing vast amounts of documents. Changing its title, and its administration, several times, the tracing service was finally given the name of International Tracing Service, to be run under the auspices of the ICRC and funded by Germany. To these buildings, in the late 1940s and early 1950s, came all the documents concerning German and non-German civilians who were incarcerated in concentration and labour camps, or non-Germans who had been displaced. Forty-six million reference cards relating to approximately fifteen million people are currently held. In the mid 1990s, fifty years after the end of the war, enquiries continue to arrive as former inmates and their relations grow old and need certificates to prove their identity in order to claim pensions, or simply because they want clarity before they die. The German government continues to pay out of their War Reparation Fund for the activities of the International Tracing Service. 212,512 enquiries were registered in 1994 from fifty-seven different countries.

Throughout the world, individual Red Cross Societies continue to receive similar queries as to the fate of people who vanished over half a century ago. The need for records of all kinds, documents, birth certificates, photographs and wills, has long been recognized as essential in the struggle made by refugees to come to terms with their past lives, and construct new ones.

After the war, the British Red Cross Society continued the war-time work carried out by its Foreign Relations Department. For a while, the work was slow. Refugees, fearing trouble, held back from making enquiries, while progress was often hampered by lack of records. By the early 1960s, however, with a slight thaw in relations with the eastern European countries, the British Red Cross Tracing Department was able to put over ten thousand families separated by the war in touch with each other. Its philosophy has remained what it always was: that whatever other tracing needs arise – and there have been many – people divided by the Second World War should never be forgotten. The stories of some of these people are told in this book.

The humanitarian world might be forgiven for imagining that the aftermath of the Second World War would see an end for ever for the need for tracing services. So many people dead; so many lost. It was not so. Even as the fighting ended, new conflicts produced the same need for news, for contact, for reassurance. Each war, each conflict, each revolution and internal confrontation, has produced prisoners and parted people from their families and relations. Even as troubles begin, so the ICRC in Geneva and the tracing services in the National Red Cross and Red Crescent Societies brace themselves for the inevitable flood of enquiries. First came the civil war in Greece, immediately after the end of the Second World War; then Palestine, Korea, Algeria, Suez, Vietnam, Hungary, Salvador, Iran and Iraq, Afghanistan – the list is never ending. In early 1995, the ICRC announced that it was willing to accept tracing enquiries arising out of the conflict in former Yugoslavia. The British Red Cross Tracing Service estimates that even were the fighting in former Yugoslavia to stop now, there would still be tracing of missing soldiers and civilians well into the twenty-first century. The wars go on, as do the disasters – for earthquakes, floods and hurricanes disperse people just as surely as wars do. And with the coming down of the Berlin wall, and the break up of the Soviet Union, have come new archives, new lists of names, new records dating back to the days when 3.3 million Germans were made prisoners of war in Russia and over a million never returned.

Certainty, as Henry Dunant perceived, is essential for peace of mind. Better, far, to know beyond all possible doubt that someone is dead, than to wait indefinitely in hope and apprehension. There is no image of tracing more haunting than the posters circulated by the tracing service in Germany in the years following the Second World War. When the index cards had all been filled in, when survivors and displaced people had at last all been registered and the numbers of those still missing calculated, the tracers came to the conclusion that at least two hundred and ninety-eight thousand children were still missing and unaccounted for, or had been separated from their parents. Thirty-three thousand of them were foundlings, so young they did not know their own names. Photographs of these small figures, some no more than two or three years old, some clutching stuffed animals, others wearing woolly hats or bonnets, most with fair hair and blue eyes, were printed and sent out to hang in railway stations, at bus stops, and in post offices. 'Has anyone' read the caption, 'seen this child?'

Caroline Moorehead is currently writing a history of the ICRC

An End to the Nightmares

The soldiers don't knock on the door: they kick it off its hinges. Alex and his father are forced out of the house at gunpoint. The snow crunches under their feet as they are marched into a small, dimly lit square where the other men from the village are standing, shivering. Whether from cold or from fear, Alex doesn't know.

A German guard shouts at them, in Polish: the men shuffle into a ragged line. Somehow, Alex finds himself at the end of it, slightly separate from the others.

Another order, this time in German. Alex sees the soldiers aim their rifles at the pathetic little line. Time stands still. Alex turns towards his father to bid him a silent goodbye. The older man is staring straight ahead.

The silence is shattered by a volley of gunfire.

Alex hears a bullet slam into a tree behind him. Instinctively, he turns and runs into the night, somehow dodging the bullets that shower all around.

When he reaches the edge of the village, he turns and looks back. There, in the gloomy light of a solitary street lamp, he can just make out a pile of bodies slumped in the blood-stained snow.

'*Ojciec*!' he cries. '*Ojciec*! *Ojciec*!' And then he runs like the wind away from the gruesome sight. He doesn't know where he is going. He simply runs and runs . . .

'It's all right, Alex! It's all right.'

Alex wakes up with a start. His pyjamas are wet with sweat. His wife is cradling him in her arms.

'It's all right,' she says again. 'Sh! It's all right! You've been having the nightmare again.'

Alex clings on to her like a frightened child seeking comfort from its mother.

'Sh!' she says soothingly. 'I know! I know!'

'Always the same!' Alex sobs. 'Always the same nightmare.'

Who knows how many men and women faced makeshift Nazi firing squads as the Germans tightened their grip on Poland and other east European countries during the Second World War? Alex was one of the lucky ones. He escaped, but his terrifying experience haunted him relentlessly.

After the war, he made his way to Britain where, like a quarter of a million other refugees, he was offered a fresh start.

It was tough for the nineteen-year-old lad. He was ill-educated and spoke little English. He survived by doing odd jobs, moving from place to place until he eventually settled in Sheffield. There he found work as a carpenter, and met and married Katerina, a fellow Polish refugee.

He tried to put the past firmly behind him, but he could never forget the night of terror when he had faced the Nazi rifles: his nightmares made sure of that.

Katerina understood. She had her own dreadful memories. Her father, too, had been shot during the German occupation of Poland. Alex and Katerina often spoke of their fathers and promised themselves that one day they would return and find their graves.

But what Alex didn't know was that his father was still alive! On that night of nightmares, the first Nazi bullets had ripped into Janos Kochanowski's leg. As he slumped forwards, the men on either side of him fell dead, protecting him from the gunfire.

He had no idea how long he lay there, hovering between consciousness and coma. He had vague memories of being dragged away from the carnage and, when he came to, he found himself being cared for by Polish partisans.

His first thoughts were for his son. But when he asked about him . . . 'No one survived but you,' he was told. 'We buried all the dead.'

Janos thought his world had come to an end. But as time passed, he knew he had to get on with his life even though he dreaded going to bed at night: for his sleep too was tormented by vivid nightmares of the night he had faced the firing squad and lost his son.

By the 1980s, with the gradual thaw in East-West relations, Polish refugees were able to go home to visit friends and relatives. Among them was Jozef Morsztyn, an acquaintance of Janos from before the war. Towards the end of his holiday, he called at his flat. They chatted nostalgically about the old days. Then Jozef asked quite casually, 'How's Alex these days?'

There was a stunned silence before Janos haltingly

told Jozef what had happened on that appalling night in 1942.

'That's impossible!' Jozef cried. 'I was in digs with him in Glasgow in 1949. We used to go boxing together. He was good.'

Janos couldn't believe his ears! Alex had survived the Nazi bullets!

A few days later, a letter from Janos was delivered to the Polish Red Cross in Warsaw. His plea was a familiar one: 'Please find my son before it is too late. I am now eighty-five and if, by some miracle, he *is* still alive, he is all that I have.' The only clue he could give was the Glasgow address where Alex had shared a room with Jozef Morsztyn. The Polish Red Cross passed the request on to the British Red Cross Tracing Service in London, asking them to do what they could to find Alex Kochanowski.

Glasgow has changed out of all recognition since the war: huge areas have been cleared to accommodate cross-city motorways; street after street of slum housing in the city centre has been demolished, their occupants resettled in vast, anonymous housing estates built on the outskirts. It seemed unlikely to Jenny McDowell, the Red Cross volunteer who was asked to look after the Glasgow end of the case, that what had probably been a run-down boarding house would have escaped the redevelopers' bulldozers.

However, the building still stood; a handsome almost imposing villa on the south side of the city. And, what was even more surprising, the woman who had owned it in 1949 still lived in it.

She asked Jenny in and offered her a cup of tea. When Jenny explained why she was there, the old woman shook her head. 'I must have had twenty, maybe thirty people here after the war. I haven't kept in touch with any of them.'

'All we know about him is that he lived here,' said Jenny. 'Oh, and that he was a keen boxer.'

A flicker of recognition came into the old lady's eyes. 'Ah, I think I know the one you mean.'

She eased herself out of her armchair, hobbled across to the fireplace and took a framed photograph down from the mantelpiece. Jenny looked at the picture.

'But this is a dog!' She was unable to keep the puzzlement from her voice.

'I know that,' the old lady said sharply. 'You see, my husband was keen on boxing, too, and although he didn't speak Polish, he and your Alex grew quite friendly. A few weeks after Alex left, Cass, my husband, bought me a pup, and we called it Alex.'

'You were that fond of him?' said Jenny.

'Yes, but it was more because the dog was a boxer that we named him after the Polish boxer.'

'Do you have any idea where he went when he left Glasgow?'

The old lady thought for a moment or two. 'North of England somewhere, I think. Liverpool was it? Or Sheffield? Yes, that's it. He said he was going to Sheffield.'

Betty Kenny, a Red Cross volunteer in Sheffield, was asked to take over the case. She knew from experience that sometimes the most effective way of tracing a 'missing' person is the most obvious: the telephone directory. So she sat down and laboriously went through all the local directories looking for the name Alex Kochanowski.

There was no Alex Kochanowski listed. So Betty looked again, this time for anyone with a similar name. She found an Alexandre Chokonowski who lived a short bus ride away. It could just be that this was the man she was looking for.

As she made her way to the house, Betty ran through the questions she would ask if she thought Alexandre Chokonowski and Alex Kochanowski were the same person. She would probe him very gently and, only if she was absolutely certain that he was the man she was looking for, would she break the news that his father was still alive. She could have no idea what his reaction would be. It could be friendly, it could be abusive.

The man who came to the door was far too tall to be Alex Kochanowski. But as they talked, he told her that he had sometimes been mistaken for a man with a similar name who had gone to live in Bristol.

The Bristol Branch of the Red Cross was alerted and followed several leads but Alex Kochanowski, if he was still alive, was not living in the city, as far as the Red Cross could establish.

Meanwhile, Betty was still hard at work in Sheffield. She searched through the records of local registrars' offices, hoping to find a marriage certificate, a birth certificate, any official document bearing the name Kochanowski or something similar. The search threw up several leads, but they all proved fruitless.

Next she got in touch with Polish clubs in and around Sheffield. The clubs keep Poles in touch with one another, providing a network of information about emigré Poles all over the country. Everyone Betty spoke to was anxious to help, but no one knew the boxing Pole.

Alex had been brought up a Roman Catholic. Perhaps if he was still in Sheffield, he went to mass in one of the many Catholic churches in the city. Betty contacted every priest in the area, but again no one knew an Alex Kochanowski.

Two years had now passed since old Janos had written to the Polish Red Cross. Betty, beginning to think it was more and more unlikely that she would ever find his son, decided to have one last try. She arranged to visit all the boxing clubs in Sheffield.

When she explained why she was there, the membership secretary of one of the clubs suggested she talked to the old trainer who had been a member since the 1950s.

'Alex Kochanowski,' he said. 'Yes, I remember him. Useful fighter he was; bit long in the tooth. Now, if I'd got hold of him earlier . . .'

The old man told Betty that he had occasionally given Alex a lift home to a housing estate on the fringes of the city. 'Couldn't tell you the exact address, mind,' he said.

But Betty didn't mind. At last, she had something definite to go on.

As soon as she could, she found time to spend a day on the estate. When she got off the bus, she literally bumped into a milkman. 'I don't suppose you've got a Pole called Alex Kochanowski on your round?' she asked, knowing deep down that she was clutching at straws.

The milkman shook his head. 'Sorry, love,' he

said. 'But there are half a dozen other milkrounds on the estate. Maybe on one of them . . .'

Betty's heart sank.

Next, she tried the newsagent's shop across the road. Her hopes soared for a moment when the girl behind the counter said they delivered papers to a man with a funny sounding name who looked as if he'd been a boxer. But when she looked in the book, the name she'd been thinking of was nothing like Alex Kochanowski.

Betty lost count of the number of people she talked to that morning, until just before lunchtime she found herself in a small street with a shop on one corner and a pub opposite. Her hopes rose again when the shopkeeper said that he knew someone who sounded like the man Betty was searching for. 'Don't know where he lives, though. Keeps himself very much to himself.'

Betty felt her stomach churn a little. 'I'm getting warm,' she said to herself. 'I'm definitely getting warm.'

Next, she went into the pub. 'I don't suppose,' she said to the young barman, 'that you know a Pole called Alex Kochanowski. Used to be a keen boxer. Keeps himself to himself.'

The youth thought for a moment. 'Old Tom, one of my regulars, usually sits there,' he said, nodding towards an empty table. 'He used to have a Polish friend. Maybe he'd know.'

'Will he be in later?' asked Betty.

'On holiday,' said the barman. 'For two weeks.'

'In that case,' sighed Betty, writing her name and phone number on a piece of paper, 'perhaps you'd ask him to give me a ring on this number when he gets back.'

By the time she got home that day she was exhausted, but now she had a definite lead she was determined not to give up. She returned to the estate time and time again over the following two weeks. Some of the people she asked were kind and courteous; some were suspicious and offensive. No one knew a Pole called Alex Kochanowski.

And then one day her phone rang: it was the barman. Her heart quickened when she heard that Tom's Polish friend was called Alex Kochanowski. 'He hasn't seen him for ages though,' the barman said, 'but he knows where he lives . . .'

The next morning Betty found herself walking towards a spruce-looking house not far from the pub. Her knock was answered by a handsome woman. Betty explained that she was from the Red Cross and had been asked by colleagues in Poland to trace a man called Alex Kochanowski who, she thought, may be living at this address.

The woman opened the door wide and beckoned Betty inside. 'Is it good news?' There was a note of suspicion in the woman's voice.

'I hope so,' said Betty. 'But I'm afraid I have to make sure that your husband . . .' she let an unspoken question mark hang in the air. The woman nodded. '. . . that your husband is the man I'm looking for before I can tell you what it is.'

'He hasn't been well,' the woman's voice was soft. 'Not for some time. And he's lost a lot of his English. I'll have to translate for you. Is that all right?'

Betty nodded as she was shown into the living-room. The man sitting in a chair struggled to his feet as the two women entered, but when his wife said something to him in Polish he slumped back in his chair.

Very gently, through Katerina, Betty asked the man if he had been born in Grygodny in Poland in 1927. He nodded.

Had he lived in Glasgow? Again he nodded.

And had he been a keen boxer? Yes, he had.

When she was certain that the man was Janos Kochanowski's son, she asked Katerina to tell her husband that it had been his father who had asked the Red Cross to trace his son.

When Alex heard his father's name, he began to thump the table beside his chair again and again with his fist, sending books and papers flying in all directions.

'Is this a joke?' The woman spat the words out. 'Alex's father was shot by the Germans. He's dead!' Betty tried to calm her, but the words tumbled from the woman's mouth: Alex was the only one to escape; he had never got over it . . .

Alex stopped banging the table. He clasped his hands over his ears and began to sob terribly. Katerina stopped shouting and tried to comfort him.

Almost as if she was talking to a child, Betty told Katerina that Janos had not been killed. He had been badly injured, but he had survived. He was alive.

'My father! Alive!' cried Alex, when Katerina translated the words for him. 'It's not true. I saw him. Dead!'

Betty took an envelope embossed with the famous Red Cross symbol from her bag and laid it on the table.

Alex's hands trembled as he unfolded the letter he

drew from the envelope. He shook his head in disbelief as he read, over and over again, the name and address of the father he thought had been dead for almost forty years.

'Why did he wait so long?' asked Katerina. 'Why didn't he try to find us when the war was over?'

Betty told her about Jozef Morsztyn and how he had gone back to Poland two years before: 'It was only then that he knew Alex could still be alive. The first thing he did was to ask the Polish Red Cross to try to trace him.'

Katerina began to apologise for having lost her temper. 'Please,' said Betty. 'I quite understand.'

Betty went back to the house three or four weeks later, to see how Alex was coping with the trauma of finding out that his father was still alive.

Katerina greeted her with a warm hug. 'Alex is much better,' she said. 'So much better.'

Betty saw that for herself a few moments later when she went into the living-room. Alex grasped her hand. 'Ah! Red Cross. Red Cross!' he said over and over again, squeezing a photograph into her hand.

'It arrived yesterday,' explained Katerina.

Betty looked at the face of an old man whose shy smile had been caught by the camera.

'*Ojciece Pana syje,*' she heard Alex whisper.

She looked enquiringly at Katerina.

'Father is alive.'

For Alex and Janos Kochanowski the nightmare was over.

From Lithuania – With Difficulty

In April 1957, Red Cross volunteers in Wales were puzzled to read press reports that Ivan Sienkiewicz's daughter had been given an exit visa by Soviet authorities and had been reunited with her father in Wales. They were surprised because they had been working for months to help Ivan's daughter leave Lithuania, and they had constantly failed.

After checking with him they found that the young woman who had been allowed to leave her home was not the girl they had been trying to get out of Vilnius. Unknown to them, Ivan had another daughter, Nina, by his first wife; it was Nina who had featured in the press reports and who was now living in Wales with Ivan and his second wife, Rosa.

At first, Rosa was pleased that Ivan had his daughter with him, but it wasn't long before she started to feel resentful. Why should Nina have been allowed to come to Britain while Maria was still in Lithuania, with no sign that the Soviet authorities would ever let her leave . . .

Ivan Sienkiewicz had been in the Polish army when German troops crossed the border on 1 September, 1939. Ivan and thousands of other Polish soldiers were taken prisoner in the early days of the war. When Rosa heard what had happened to her husband, she fled to her parents in Lithuania.

Reunited!

Somehow Ivan escaped and joined his wife in Vilnius. In 1940, their baby, Maria, was born. When Maria was a few months old, Lithuania was incorporated into the Soviet Union which systematically began to move Polish families into Russia. For years, even when she was perfectly safe, Rosa's sleep was constantly disturbed by dreadful dreams of the day she and Ivan had been forced at gunpoint to board Russian trucks and driven to separate concentration camps. The police had orders to take little Maria, too, but when they came to arrest the family, the baby was gravely ill: she was left behind with her grandparents who were too old to be of any use to the Russians.

Like many Poles, Ivan had an extraordinary war. In 1941, following an agreement between the Soviet and Polish governments, Ivan was released from his camp and in 1942 he joined the Polish Army in Russia. When his unit was posted to defend Russia's oil fields on the border with Persia, he managed to trace Rosa and got her to a camp in Persia. Just over nine months later, she gave birth to a son, Peter. Rosa and Peter were then moved to a refugee camp in India. In 1944, Ivan was badly wounded fighting with allied troops in Italy; and two years later, he came to Britain with the Polish Resettlement Corps.

Given the circumstances after the war, it is little short of a miracle that it took only a year for Ivan to get permission for his wife and son to leave the refugee camp in India and join him in the UK. They settled in Wales. He would have liked nothing better than for Maria to come to Wales, too, but he knew full well that this was impossible.

Rosa and Ivan wrote to Maria and her grandparents as often as they could. They told them about life in Wales, about their house, Ivan's job and, of course, about Peter, the brother Maria had never seen. The replies, when they were eventually received, were extremely guarded for no one knew which letters were read by censors and which went unopened. But at least Rosa and Ivan knew that their daughter was alive and was being well looked after.

In 1956 the Sienkiewiczs' world fell apart when Peter was killed in a road accident. At first Rosa and Ivan were numb with grief: they found the strength to get through the funeral and the dark days that followed, and they were just starting to pick up the pieces of their shattered lives when they were struck by another bombshell. Maria wrote from Lithuania with the terrible news that her grandmother was losing her sight and was rapidly becoming too ill to look after herself, never mind a sixteen-year-old teenager. 'Grandad has to spend most of his time caring for her,' she wrote. 'We both think that the best thing would be if I come and live with you in England . . .'

'. . . if I come and live with you in England', Rosa and Ivan read the words over and over again. They had no idea how to begin to go about getting Maria out of Lithuania. In desperation they turned to their local Red Cross Branch which contacted the British Red Cross headquarters in London to see if anything could be done.

The Red Cross advised Ivan and Rosa to write to the Foreign Office applying for a Statutory Declaration, a document giving official sanction for Maria to be allowed to settle in Britain in the event of her being permitted to leave Lithuania.

The Declaration was quickly issued along with a promise that if, and it was a huge if, the Russians gave Maria her exit papers, the British Embassy in Moscow would immediately issue a British entry visa.

When Maria heard what was happening she wrote such an enthusiastic letter to her mother that for the first time in months, Rosa found herself smiling. But four months later Maria was still in Vilnius. The Declaration had been sent to Moscow, but there was no sign of the girl being allowed to leave.

Rosa refused to believe that the Russians would not let her daughter go. She was so certain that Maria would soon be with her that she wrote to her father asking him to begin to make the necessary travel arrangements. She had no idea what this involved. If Maria was allowed to leave Vilnius, she would have to fly to East Berlin, be escorted to the British sector and then flown to London. Rosa's father was far too frail to apply for all the visas she would need, but Rosa was so persistent that he spent what little savings he had to pay a lawyer to do it for him.

Back in Wales, Rosa was becoming more and more agitated. In December, six months after the Foreign Office papers had been sent to Lithuania, the British Red Cross wrote to the Soviet Red Cross in Moscow asking if they could confirm that all the proper procedures had been followed for the application of an exit visa. Two months later, the Russians replied promising to help, and in July, the Red Cross in London heard from them that Maria had been given permission to leave Lithuania by the end of the month.

Rosa was overjoyed. But a few days later news

came through that there had been a change of plan. The Russians were insisting that Maria had to finish her education before she would be allowed to leave.

Maria and Ivan began to bombard the Russians with letters: they even wrote to Nikita Kruschev, the Russian leader, but to no avail. In January 1958, the Soviet Red Cross wrote to London that it had become clear that Maria would not be allowed to leave Lithuania. It seemed that there was nothing more the British Red Cross could do but thank their fellow workers at the Soviet Red Cross for all that had been done, and express the hope that one day things may change.

Rosa became more and more bitter about her life: her flight from Poland; her forced separation from her baby; the Russian labour camp; the journey to Persia; the refugee camp in India; Peter's death; and now this. She lost interest in life. She started to neglect herself and fell into a deep depression.

The newspapers got hold of the story. The Red Cross were worried about the press coverage when they saw it on the front page of *The Daily Telegraph*, as sometimes this had an adverse effect in communist countries on the efforts under way.

A week or two later, quite out of the blue, Ivan telephoned the Welsh Branch of the Red Cross asking if anyone there could confirm a letter he had received from Maria saying that she was about to be given her passport and exist visa. Within days, the Red Cross in Moscow verified this: Maria was to be allowed to leave Lithuania on 15 September.

The appointed day came and went with Maria still in Lithuania. Rosa began to think that it had all been a misunderstanding: the Soviet authorities must have changed their mind. As the days turned into weeks and with still no sign of Maria, Rosa was on the verge of a nervous breakdown.

In Lithuania things were just as bad, if not worse, for Maria. Every day she was told that she would have her papers and be on an East Berlin flight within a matter of hours. Her suitcase was packed, all she could do was wait and pray. Eventually, on 18 October, more than four weeks after she had first been told to get ready, she was taken to a military air strip on the outskirts of Vilnius and put aboard a plane bound for East Germany.

The aircraft had already landed and Maria was being looked after by the British Command in West Berlin when word was received in Wales that she had left Vilnius. A Red Cross volunteer drove Rosa and Ivan to London Airport where they arrived just in time to see Maria's plane land.

It was not until they had held her in their arms that they really believed that the daughter they had not seen for seventeen years was with them at last. Soon they were on their way home, looking forward to getting to know Maria for the first time.

The family could not have known it, but in Wales, London and Moscow Red Cross workers too felt some of this joy, mixed with pride in the fact that each was a link in this Red Cross world-wide humanitarian chain.

It was one of the British Red Cross Tracing Service's earliest successes – the seemingly impossible had been achieved.

Recalled to Life

Sometimes the Red Cross do more than reunite families separated by wars. Sometimes they bring people back to life . . .

One day, in the early 1970s, Voyzek Schultz was visiting a friend, a short-term voluntary patient in a psychiatric hospital near his home in Wales. When he was about to leave, he spotted a man at the other end of the day room, slowly rocking his chair backwards and forwards, staring blankly ahead as if there was an opaque wall between him and the rest of the world.

'Who's that man over there?' he asked one of the nurses.

The nurse looked round. 'Frederic, do you mean?' she said. 'Frederic Krasinski.'

'He looks as if he's in a world of his own.'

'He is,' the nurse went on. 'He's been here for twenty-three years and never says a word. Even if he did, we wouldn't understand. The doctor said he's Ukrainian. At least we think he is.'

Voyzek knew that most Ukrainians have a smattering of Polish, so when he was leaving, he smiled at the simple-looking man and said 'Goodbye' in Polish to him.

The man's face remained quite expressionless.

The next time Voyzek went to the hospital, he said

'Hello' to Frederic Krasinski, again in Polish. Frederic stopped rocking, looked at the stranger and mumbled something Voyzek could not quite make out.

From then on, whenever Voyzek went to see his friend, he always tried to find a minute or two to spend with the poor Ukrainian. Gradually the barrier between him and the rest of the world came down.

Unable to communicate with anyone for many years, Frederic found talking difficult. But Voyzek persevered. Week by week he very gently drew Frederic out of his shell, never rushing him, never agitating him, never forcing him to speak.

Language was still a hurdle, for Frederic didn't speak much Polish and Voyzek had no Ukrainian. Frederic often had little idea what Voyzek was saying to him, but slowly, week by week, month by month, the kindly Pole pieced together Frederic's story.

He had been in the Free Polish Army and when the war came to an end had found himself in Russia. Somehow, he couldn't remember how or why, he had made his way to Persia. Then, he thought he had been sent to Canada, but things hadn't worked out for him there, or wherever it was, and the next thing he remembered was being in Britain, in the hospital where Voyzek had met him.

One day, from out of nowhere, Frederic mentioned that he had a sister living in Russia.

'She's probably dead by now,' he said. 'I don't know when I last saw her.'

Voyzek knew about the work the Red Cross did. He suggested getting in touch with its Tracing

Service, asking them to try to find Frederic's sister.

Frederic was silent for a moment or two. Then he nodded his head slowly, and said something Voyzek didn't understand.

'What was that?' he asked, puzzled.

Frederic repeated the word. 'That's where she lived,' he mumbled.

Voyzek wrote two letters: one to the Red Cross in London, and another addressed to the woman care of the post office of the village she had lived in. Maybe she was still there and whoever ran the post office may know her address.

At the end of August 1973, the Red Cross passed Voyzek's letter to the Red Cross in Moscow but told him not to expect miracles. At this time thousands of tracing enquiries were being received.

There was no reply to the letter Voyzek wrote to Frederic's sister, but four months later the Soviet Red Cross wrote to say that Frederic's sister, Clara, had left the village long before, and they had traced her at her new address. And there was even more good news. They had traced another sister, Natasha.

When Frederic was told that he had not one, but two living sisters, he was overjoyed. Voyzek told his wife later that it was as if someone had switched on a warm, soft light inside the old man.

As the days passed, it seemed to everyone at the hospital that Frederic, like Dickens's Dr Manette, had been recalled to life. His doctor wrote to the Red Cross two months later thanking them for what they had done and telling them that the change in Frederic was little short of miraculous. He was alert and, for the first time in years, was showing an interest in what was happening around him.

He had his photograph taken and sent it to Clara along with a letter he had hesitantly dictated in Polish to Voyzek, asking his sisters for their photographs in exchange. Voyzek translated Frederic's words into English, and it was with a faltering hand that Frederic wrote 'Dear Clara' at the top and then painstakingly signed his name at the bottom. The letter was sent to the Red Cross in Moscow for them to forward to Clara and Natasha. Although the contents were quite incomprehensible to them and had to be translated, they could see the enormous effort that their brother had made to contact them and sign the letter in his own hand.

Shortly afterwards, Clara sent photographs of herself and Natasha direct to Frederic at the hospital. The letter wrapped around them was written in a curious mixture of Ukrainian and Russian, but it was obvious from the ease with which Frederic read it, that this was his native dialect. Little wonder no one had been able to communicate with him other than in the few words of Polish he had.

Frederic was unable to write. When he replied to Clara's letter, he had to ask Voyzek to write in Polish, and then someone in the Soviet Red Cross translated for Clara and Natasha.

A few weeks later, Frederic received another letter from Clara. When he read it, he burst into tears and began to babble incomprehensively to himself. Natasha, it turned out, was in hospital.

The doctor was concerned that the news would undo all the good work Voyzek had done, but eventually Frederic calmed down and asked his friend to write another letter.

A month passed: no news. Another month: still

nothing. At the end of the third month Voyzek asked the Red Cross if they could find out what was happening.

They wrote back within three weeks with the devastating news. Natasha had died in hospital. Clara, not knowing how to break the news to Frederic, had put off writing to him. But now, desperate to see her brother again, she had begged the Soviet Red Cross to bring him to her in Russia where they could spend what time was left to them together.

Everyone knew that this was virtually impossible. However, it was thought best for the sake of Frederic's mental health to consider the possibility of a reunion.

The Red Cross promised that, at a time they judged appropriate, they would contact the Soviet Embassy in London. In the meantime, the hospital administrator made enquiries and established that Frederic's army pension could be paid to him in Russia. But the Soviet Red Cross worker explained to Clara that it would take months, maybe years, for Frederic to be allowed into Russia – if at all.

By now, Clara was desperate to see her long-lost brother. She suggested applying for an exit visa herself so that she could visit Frederic in Wales. The Red Cross, with their long experience of dealing with Soviet bureaucracy, told her that this could damage what fragile chance there was of getting Frederic into Russia.

The British Red Cross's main concern was that, in the unlikely event of Frederic being allowed to go and live with his sister, he would find it impossible to adjust, having been institutionalised for so long.

They were reassured by what the hospital told them.

Frederic, by now, was a changed man. He was enjoying outings and holidays at the seaside. Despite the language problem, he was getting on well with other long-term patients. Even better, his doctors were convinced that if, as everyone suspected, Frederic's application was rejected, he would be able to accept his fate without relapsing into his previous depression.

Sadly, three years after the Red Cross approached the Soviet Embassy in London, Frederic's application was rejected. Clara and Frederic were bitterly disappointed, but they vowed to stay in touch. Frederic still had to dictate his letters and, as before, someone on the other side translated for Clara.

At first it was Voyzek who acted as scribe, but his health began to fail, and the gaps between his visits grew longer and longer. Eventually the Red Cross asked another Polish volunteer to do the job.

When Frederic died, aged eighty-seven, in 1984, the Red Cross assumed they could close his twenty-year-old file, but three years later they were touched to receive a request from the Soviet Red Cross asking where he had been buried. Before she had died in 1986, Clara had made her family promise that should any of them ever visit Britain, they would find Frederic's grave and pay tribute to an uncle who had been recalled to life.

The Day I Found Myself

Helga Kepler runs a successful business in the fashion industry, has a beautiful house, charming husband and handsome son. She's attractive, confident and well groomed. It's unlikely that anyone meeting her today would realize that her life had started in poverty and abuse, that for years she was driven by a deep obsession to find her mother, a woman of whom she had no memory whatsoever.

All she knew was that her mother was an Austrian called Elsa and that she had been a farmworker. She didn't know that Elsa loved going out and, whenever she could, had headed for the nearest town to dance the night away, or sit in a café, flirting with the good-looking men who flocked around her.

In 1937 she became pregnant but had the baby boy to whom she gave birth adopted when he was a few days old. A year later she set her cap at a handsome young man called Hans who caught her flighty eye.

Their affair was as brief as it was passionate. Within weeks, Elsa had become bored with her good-looking young beau. Soon the pair were bickering. Then the squabbles became full-scale rows and as quickly as the affair had begun, it was over.

A few weeks later, Elsa began to feel sick in the mornings. She knew very well what that could mean,

39

but even so she was horrified when her doctor confirmed that she was pregnant again.

Hans had to be the father, but when she went to break the news to him, she was flabbergasted to find that he had been swept off his feet by another girl whom he had already married and who was expecting his child.

Elsa's daughter, Helga, was born in February 1939. Elsa decided that this time she would keep the baby so she took her back to the farm where she worked. It wasn't long before Hans heard about the child and went to see her and her mother.

He was disgusted with what he found. Gone was the lively, high-spirited girl he had loved: there were bags under her eyes, her skin had hardened and her hair hung in rats' tails around her once-rosy face.

With hindsight, it is obvious that Elsa was suffering from extremely serious post-natal depression. But in Hans's eyes, she had totally transformed beyond all recognition. Even worse, little Helga lay asleep, obviously unchanged, in a makeshift cot that smelled of soiled sheets. Hans was furious. He ranted at the poor woman, accusing her of being unfit to call herself a mother. Elsa, in no frame of mind to defend herself, sat in sullen silence and made no move to comfort the baby when she started to cry. Long after Hans left, Elsa lay on her bed, indifferent to Helga's screams. She could cry to kingdom come for all Elsa cared.

She was amazed when Hans came back.

'What do you want?' she said.

'Helga! I've arranged for her to be looked after by the Carlssons.'

Why not? Elsa asked herself. Nobody cared about

her, and she didn't care about Helga. Let someone else look after her. And she did nothing to stop Hans take Helga from her cot and felt nothing as she watched him take her away.

Within weeks, German troops invaded Poland. Hans, like most young Austrian men, was dragooned into the Nazi army, leaving his family behind.

Helga grew to be a surly, unruly child, always in trouble. Frau Carlsson despaired of her. 'Mark my words,' she would say to the headstrong girl. 'If you don't behave, we'll send you away.' Helga's response was to simply shrug her stubborn little shoulders.

But one day, when Helga was nine, Frau Carlsson had had enough. She told the social services that Helga was quite beyond her control and that she could no longer look after her. A few days later, Helga found herself in the care of Conrad and Myrtel Braun, a farming couple who lived some distance away. It turned out that the Brauns didn't want a child; they wanted an unpaid labourer and treated Helga little better than a slave.

For years, when she was not at school, Helga was forced to work from dawn to dusk. And if there was pressing work to be done on the farm, she was kept away from school until it was finished. She put up with abuse and ill-treatment for five years. But night after night as she lay in her bed she cried her eyes out, and rued the way she had ignored Frau Carlsson's repeated warnings.

By the time she was fourteen she had had enough. Late one night, when she knew that the Brauns would be asleep, she wrapped what little she owned in a sheet and crept from the house, determined somehow to make her way back to the Carlssons.

A few days later she was found, suffering from exhaustion and shivering from the cold, slumped in a shop doorway in Wels, a small town not far from Linz. She was taken to a nearby convent where the sisters took her in and put her to work doing small tasks around the convent. In return she was allowed to attend the convent school. It proved to be a turning point for Helga.

For the first time in her life, Helga felt that someone cared for her. The nuns were serious but not above enjoying a hearty laugh, strict but not cruel, devout but not overly pious, and above all they were full of kindness. Helga came to love them dearly.

For their part, the nuns were quick to spot that Helga was a bright and talented little seamstress as well. Frau Braun had seen to that, bullying her into doing all the sewing that had to be done and standing over her until it was done to her complete satisfaction.

The young girl took quickly to embroidery when the nuns showed her how to do it, and later developed a talent for dressmaking. When she left the convent school, Helga went on to college to study dress design.

It was at about this time that she began to feel the need to meet her mother. At first it was just a whim, but the more she thought about it, the more the idea took hold of her. The whim grew into a desire, and the desire into a determination that one day she *would* look her mother in the face and ask why she had abandoned her.

The first thing she did was to contact her local records office.

What was her mother's name? Elsa Schauffus.

What was her last address? Helga had no idea.

When was she born? Again, Helga had no answer.

The woman at the records office was firm but kind. With so little to go on, it would be like looking for a needle in a haystack. She would do what she could, but . . .

When Helga went back to the office a week or two later, the same woman told her that they had found an Elsa Schauffus on their files who was the right age to have been Helga's mother, but they had no idea where she was now. Countless files had been lost or destroyed during the war: they had no way of knowing if she was dead or alive. But there was some good news. The birth and adoption details of a boy born to Elsa Schauffus had survived. Perhaps if Helga contacted the agency, they could put her in touch with him.

A half-brother? This came as a complete surprise and Helga was overjoyed to know that she may find some family. She straightaway wrote to the adoption agency and waited for what seemed like an eternity for a reply.

When it came, Helga couldn't believe her eyes. Elsa had had a son called Fritz. He had been adopted by a family in Linz. And even better, they knew where he was living now.

Fritz was thunderstruck to receive a letter from a woman claiming to be his half-sister. But his interest was aroused enough for him to arrange to meet her.

What do you say to a twenty-year-old sister you have never met? Do you call her Helga? Fraulein?

How do you greet a twenty-two-year-old brother of whose existence you were quite unaware until a few weeks before? An embrace? A handshake?

The stiff formality of the first few minutes in each other's company quickly gave way to shy curiosity. The two quickly warmed to each other and were soon talking as if they had been childhood friends catching up after years apart.

The only shadow for Helga fell when Fritz told her that he had tried to trace their mother a few years before but had drawn a blank. Now, he liked to think that she had been killed in the war rather than being out there, beyond his reach. Helga didn't try to hide her tears when Fritz suggested she did the same. 'Try. Please try,' he said. 'It takes time, but it makes the pain easier to bear. I promise.'

Not long after she had met her brother, Helga decided to leave Austria. She took a job as an *au pair* in London and arrived with one suitcase containing all she owned. Try as she might to follow Fritz's advice, she couldn't bring herself to believe her mother was dead. She had to know one way or the other.

A few months after she had arrived in Britain, Helga was struck by such an obvious idea that she kicked herself for not thinking about it earlier. Why not try to trace her mother through Frau Carlsson, her first foster-mother?

She wrote to the house where she had, she recalled

with a shiver, behaved so appallingly. Miraculously, she received a reply – not from Frau Carlsson, but from the family who now lived there. Helga's heart raced as she read that her foster-mother, now an elderly woman, lived in an old folk's home on the outskirts of Linz.

Helga asked the couple whose baby she was looking after if she could go home for a few days and when they agreed, spent the last of her savings to pay for the trip.

When Gerda Carlsson was told that the attractive young woman who had come all the way from England to see her was the child she had fostered so many years before, she burst into tears. Not tears of happiness, but tears of remorse, for she had come to regret sending the child away no matter how much trouble she had caused.

Helga was quick to calm her. She realised she had been an impossible child, she said. No one could blame her foster-mother for what had happened. Helga understood.

Gerda wiped away her tears. When Helga asked her if she knew anything about where her natural mother had gone – the town or city, anything – the old lady shook her head: 'It was all so long ago,' she sighed. 'So long ago.'

Gerda promised to see her old foster-mother every day before she returned to London. On one of her visits, another of the old ladies in the home happened to overhear Helga mention Elsa Schauffus.

'Elsa Schauffus?' she croaked. 'Elsa Anderssen you mean. At least that's what she was calling herself last time I heard of her!'

Slowly, it emerged that shortly after Helga had

been taken from her Elsa had come to live in Linz. She had married a Michael Anderssen, but had divorced him in 1948. No one had heard of her for years; she may be dead, or she could still be living in the town.

As soon as she was back in London, Helga wrote to the British Red Cross, begging them to do what they could to trace her mother. 'Being alone for such a long time has become a big dark mountain,' she wrote. 'I have to know if my mother has been alive all this time.'

The Austrian Red Cross started with a search through records in Linz which threw up several women who may or may not have been Helga's mother. Each had to be checked with the customary Red Cross patience and tact, asking if one of them had given up a baby boy for adoption in 1937, and given birth to a daughter two years later.

It wasn't long before they had traced Helga's mother who had married again. Elsa was dumb-struck when she heard it had been her daughter who had asked the Red Cross to search for her.

Unable to speak, she shook her head when she was told that if she wanted to keep Helga locked in the past, the Red Cross would not divulge her address. They would, if necessary, explain that Elsa was alive but had no interest in contact with her daughter. Eventually Elsa found her voice. 'No,' she whispered. 'Tell her where I am.'

When the news was broken to Helga in London her initial reaction was to take the next flight to Austria. The Red Cross tracing officer in London, with her years of experience, urged caution. Helga had been almost obsessive in her search, and she was warned that the search was not the most difficult part. That would be trying to establish a relationship with someone who was a stranger but also her mother.

At first Helga brushed their objections aside. 'I have to see her, even if it's only once in my life,' she said. 'I have to see her now.'

It was, however, several months before she returned to Austria to meet her mother for the first time in her memory. If there was a slight hesitancy in the way they hugged each other, if their conversation was more than a little faltering at first, that's only understandable. So, too, were the tears that were soon flowing down both women's faces.

Helga heard all about her mother's life – about her not one but two marriages. About the son she had given birth to in 1937. When Helga told her that she had already met him, Elsa begged her daughter for his address. Within days, mother, son and daughter sat in the same room for the first time in their lives.

Helga had to return to London but now, with her obsession behind her, she was able to get on with her own life and plan her future. She put her dress-making skills to good use and within a few years had built up a successful fashion company. Now, married and with a child of her own, she is as happy as she is prosperous.

And Elsa? She's a lively octogenarian still living in Austria, and, with a 'boyfriend' twenty years her junior, still enjoying life to the full!

From Russia with Love

People react in different ways when the Red Cross Tracing Service makes contact with them. Some are happy, others are suspicious; some are overjoyed, others are overwhelmed. Few are indifferent.

But it seemed to Sara Conningsby, the volunteer who got in touch with Gerald Partiger on a matter of some delicacy, that he was being completely cavalier. For when contact was made one weekend, he asked her to telephone his wife with the details the following Monday. Sara felt that she couldn't do this. After all, she had been asked to trace the father of a love child, born in Russia in 1943 . . .

Shortly after the Soviet Union entered the war, in 1941, Gerald Partiger was sent on secondment to Moscow. He was billeted with a Russian family in what was by Muscovite standards a large flat in a sprawling apartment block near the British *chargé d'affaires'* office where he worked.

Soon he was part of the family, sharing with them the trials and tribulations of war-time Moscow, and it wasn't long before he found himself falling in love with the daughter of the house, a lovely girl called Irena.

He was already married, but he felt no guilt. His marriage had been in trouble almost from the start. The rift between his wife and himself widened, and by the time he was posted to Russia, the Partigers were on the brink of separation.

Irena was just as attracted to him as he was fascinated by her and they quickly became lovers. Her parents didn't mind, in fact they almost encouraged their daughter to snatch a little happiness while she could. The world was at war and who could tell how it would end.

In 1943, Irena gave birth to a daughter but before the child was a year old, Gerald was posted back to London. He neither tried to take Irena and the baby with him, nor promised to try to send for them after the war. He had enough experience of Soviet bureaucracy to know that it would be futile to try.

Irena and her parents lavished all their love on the baby, Alexandrina, and although life was at times intolerable in post-war Moscow, they made sure she lacked for little. Irena often talked about her dashing diplomat father so fondly that Alexandrina dreamed of meeting him.

And so it was in 1972, that Alexandrina, now an attractive, intelligent woman of twenty-eight, contacted the Soviet Red Cross asking if they could help her find Gerald Partiger.

In London, the letter from the Soviet Red Cross fell on Sara Conningsby's desk. Partiger is not a particularly common name so, although she had no precise date of birth, it wasn't long before Sara was able to trace him.

She wrote to him, asking if he was the Gerald Partiger who had been in Moscow during the war. If so, would he contact her at the Red Cross as there was something she would like to tell him. When she received Gerald's casual request to contact his wife,

Sara was put in a quandry. How could she possibly tell Mrs Partiger that her husband had had an affair when he was in Moscow and had fathered an illegitimate child?

She wrote that she needed to ask him for some information she felt only he could provide. Gerald was intrigued, and a few days later arranged to meet her. When he found out that his daughter by Irena was trying to get in touch with him, Gerald was delighted. His first question was, was Irena still alive? He had never forgotten her, although had not written to her or asked the British Embassy in Moscow to find out about her. He felt that to have done so may have endangered her, such was the suspicion with which Moscow viewed the West.

'You understand why I had to tell you personally?' said Sara Conningsby. 'I couldn't risk telling your wife . . .'

Gerald smiled. 'Dolly knows about Irena,' he interrupted her. 'I told her all about what happened in Russia before we got married last year.'

'Last year?'

'Yes. My first wife and I split up just after the war.'

'Oh I see,' Sara laughed. 'I thought you were being rather casual when you left that message about telling your wife.'

'Do you mind if I ask you some questions?' she went on. 'You see we have to be absolutely sure that Alexandrina is who she claims to be.'

'I'm very impressed, I must say,' Gerald said after he had told Sara one or two seemingly trivial things about Alexandrina's infancy that she could only have known from her mother.

'Impressed?'

'With the way you've handled this. So delicately.'

'We've had over a hundred years of experience,' said Sara.

The Soviet Red Cross were told that Gerald Partiger had been found, and they in turn confirmed that Irena was indeed still alive and had helped their daughter to make the enquiry.

When Gerald heard the news he was very pleased. He asked Sara if the Red Cross could help him to send his first letter. 'I've lost all my Russian,' he explained. 'But if someone in Moscow could translate these, I'd be grateful,' he said, giving Sara two letters. 'They're from Dolly and me,' he said. 'We would love it if Alexandrina could get over here for a visit somehow. She is my only child.'

'That could be difficult,' said Sara. 'But why don't you see how things go?'

Gerald thought for a moment or two, 'Or,' he mused, 'I wouldn't mind seeing Moscow again.'

Shortly afterwards Gerald received a letter written in perfect English from his daughter. She told him as much about herself as she could cram on to four sheets of paper. She was an English teacher, married with a little girl of four, and a baby on the way.

Gerald wrote back telling her about his life in England, his business, his home and, of course, about Dolly. 'I hope that one day we can all meet.'

The more he thought about them, the more he wanted to see Irena and Alexandrina. Dolly didn't take much persuasion and late in 1973, they contacted the British Red Cross to ask how to go about arranging a visit to Moscow. The Red Cross put them in touch with the official Soviet tourist office who couldn't have been more helpful. They arranged visas, flights and hotels. Gerald was warned against trying to stay with his daughter. The authorities may have been willing to allow tourists into the country, but there were strict rules on how they had to behave. Staying anywhere other than in approved hotels could be difficult for both guests and hosts.

The visit was a huge success. Any doubts Dolly may have had that her husband's feelings for Irena would be rekindled were soon dispelled. They were still obviously fond of each other because of the past they shared and their daughter. Gerald and Alexandrina hit it off immediately and Gerald became quite besotted by Alexandrina's little girl, his granddaughter.

All too soon it was time to board the Aeroflot flight bound for London. Gerald, who had never been an overtly emotional man, cried on Dolly's shoulder all the way back, and there were tears in his eyes when he told Sara Conningsby all about the trip. He cried, too, when a few years later, Alexandrina wrote with the sad news that Irena had died.

In 1982, Dolly Partiger wrote again to the British Red Cross asking for their help. In the nine years that had passed, Alexandrina had been allowed to visit Britain not once, but twice. 'I think she would have liked to have stayed,' she wrote, 'but, of course she couldn't. She's divorced now and she knows her ex-husband wouldn't let their children leave the country, even if the authorities would agree, which is unlikely.

'I've kept up the correspondence since Gerald died, and that's why I'm writing to you now. In her last letter, Drina told me she was ill. I've written time and time again, but none of my letters have been answered. I can't understand what has happened.'

The British Red Cross wrote back assuring Dolly that they would ask someone from the Soviet Red Cross to give a report on Alexandrina's health and welfare.

When the news arrived, Sara had the sad task of informing Dolly that Alexandrina had died of kidney failure, at the tragically early age of thirty-eight. Her children had gone to live with their father. That's why Dolly's letters had not been answered.

Dolly was devastated. She felt so terribly guilty that she had not tried to go to Moscow immediately when she had heard that Alexandrina was ill.

A few days later, Dolly called the Red Cross. 'I'd like the children's address. I want to keep in touch with them,' she said. 'For Gerald's sake – and Irena's.'

She is not my Sister: But I know her Face

Occasionally a Red Cross search has a bittersweet ending such as when Janine Heston asked the Red Cross Tracing Service to find her sister, Hélène. The two had been stagestruck teenagers in the 1920s and were often found in or around the small theatre of the French town in Provence where they lived.

When Janine and Hélène were offered the chance to join a touring repertory company, they jumped at it, and in 1928 found themselves in Rambouillet, a market town not far from Paris. Times were hard, box office receipts had been falling for some time. They were so bad in Rambouillet that the company decided to disband. Hélène and Janine went their separate ways – and that was the last they were to see of each other for almost fifty years.

In late spring 1940, the Germans marched into France. By the end of June they had taken Paris. A few days later, the French government accepted the terms of the Armistice dictated to them by their Nazi conquerors.

Janine, like thousands of other Frenchmen and women, joined the Resistance. She risked her life many times to help escaped prisoners of war and stranded allied servicemen to reach safety. She was sure that Hélène, wherever she may be, would be doing the same.

In 1945, Janine was in North Africa where she met and married Jeremy Heston, a major in the British army. When his tour of duty was over, he took his bride back to Britain where a few years later, Janine gave birth to their son.

She was widowed not long afterwards. With a young son to support and only a tiny army pension to live on, she returned to her first love, the stage. During the long gaps between jobs, she began to write – script outlines at first, and then screenplays. Soon she was making more money from her writing than from acting.

Janine never forgot her sister and often wondered if she had survived the war. She made several unsuccessful attempts to find her, and when each of them failed, promised herself that next time she would devote much more time to her quest. But what with bringing up her son, trying to resume her acting career, and later her script writing, she kept putting off the day.

It was not until 1976, that Janine called at the Red Cross office in London and begged them to find the sister she had last seen forty-eight years before. All she knew was Hélène's name, date of birth and that she had been an actress. With so little to go on, Janine was told, tracing Hélène was virtually impossible. But it was hard to say no to the anxious French woman, so the Red Cross agreed to see what could be done.

When the case was handed over to the French Red Cross they could find no trace of her in Rambouillet. Their best hope, they thought, was to try to trace Hélène through the theatre. And sure enough, after a year's intensive work, ploughing through agents' lists, old programmes and contacting theatres all over France, the search led them to a residential home in Avignon.

When the French Red Cross contacted the administrator of the home on Janine's behalf, he was more than happy to co-operate and gave them open access to her medical and social security records. Assured by the information the records contained, they informed Hélène that her sister in Britain had asked the Red Cross to find her. But the confused, elderly lady looked blankly into space. 'I have no sister,' she said in a monotone. 'I have never had a sister. I have no family.'

Even when all the facts were put to her, Hélène refused point blank to acknowledge Janine's existence. The British Red Cross had no choice but to explain to Janine, who had been waiting so impatiently, that although they had found Hélène, she insisted that she was an only child.

Janine's face crumpled and she broke down in tears. 'Are you sure that the woman you found is my sister?' she sobbed. 'Are you certain it's Hélène?'

'Absolutely certain!'

'Where is she?' asked Janine.

'I'm afraid we can't tell you that,' Janine was told with enormous sympathy. 'We have to respect everybody's right to confidentiality – no matter how distressing. I'm so sorry.'

Later, Janine cast her mind back to the war, to the time she had been questioned by Nazis who suspected her of being in the Resistance. She shuddered when she remembered the pain she had been forced to endure, the way the Nazis had systematically dehumanized her before, to her utter astonishment, they had let her go.

Perhaps Hélène had been tortured so badly by the Gestapo she had slammed shut the door on her past, and genuinely had no recollection of having a sister. Perhaps if she wrote to Hélène reminding her of their childhood and their days in the theatre, maybe something would trigger a memory that would unlock that door.

A few days later, Janine was back at Red Cross headquarters in London with a long, loving letter which she asked to be sent to Hélène wherever she was, along with a snapshot of herself taken before the war.

It wasn't long before she was back again, with a letter from the French Red Cross who had taken the unusual step of writing to her directly. Janine's letter had been read to Hélène several times. She had listened intently to what Janine had written, and when a nurse showed Hélène the photograph, a slow glimmer of recognition had spread across her face. 'I know the face,' she said, 'but this is not my sister. I do not have a sister.' The nurse had suggested to Hélène that she might write back to Janine, but she adamantly refused even to entertain the idea.

The French Red Cross had also written to their British colleagues with a letter from Hélène's doctor who wanted to know if Janine was strong enough to travel to France to visit her. They hoped that if Hélène was confronted with Janine face to face, she might begin to remember some of her past.

The Red Cross in London had little hesitation in putting this to Janine. She would have caught the next flight to France had it been up to her, but she was advised to wait until Hélène's doctors judged the time to be appropriate.

It was an extremely nervous Janine who, a few weeks later, was shown into the room where the sister she had not seen since 1928 was waiting. Janine took Hélène's hand and after they chatted of this and that, she very gently began to talk about herself, about the past, about having been an actress, about the war.

Hélène listened, but nothing Janine said kindled any memories of the past in her. When it was time to go, she bade the other woman an affectionate goodbye, but still refused to recognize her as her sister.

When she returned to London, Janine felt that if only she could see Hélène more often she could help her get her memory back. But she couldn't afford to travel to southern France more than once a year, maybe twice if she cut back on things. And then she thought that if, somehow, she could arrange for Hélène so be moved to a home near Calais or Boulogne, she could visit her much more often.

Naturally, she turned to the Red Cross for advice and when she heard that Hélène's doctors were willing to see what could be done, she started to make plans. Sadly, before the wheels could be put in motion, her own health began to deteriorate.

She was forced to cancel plans to go to Avignon again when she had to have surgery that left her in no condition to consider travelling any distance for the foreseeable future.

Every year from then onwards, a Christmas card from Janine arrived at the Red Cross's headquarters in Belgravia, with a small donation which volunteers knew she could ill-afford. She never completely recovered from her operation, and as she grew steadily weaker, a local Red Cross visitor was there to lend support.

Just before she died she said: 'I know that Hélène will never recognize me as her sister, but at least I know she is alive and well looked after. Bless you and your organization for your help and understanding.'

We will never know why Hélène blocked out her past so completely. Maybe she had been tortured by the Germans. Perhaps she had collaborated and was unable to live with her guilt. Whatever it was, it was erased from her memory along with the sister who had loved her so much.

Where's There's Hope . . .

The letter from the Prisoner of War Information Bureau was short and to the point.

Madam,
    In reply to your enquiry reference Y. St. MW/VC/ICT, dated the 21st June, 1948, I am directed to inform you that the Bureau has no record of Hans Schiller (born 10.4.23) either as a prisoner of war in British custody or as having died of wounds in hospital.

I am, Madam,
Your obedient Servant,

It was dated 25th June 1948.
Twenty-five years later, Hans Schiller's mother was still trying to find her soldier son.

One day in late 1944 when allied troops were advancing through Belgium, Hans Schiller, a medical orderly from Hanover attached to the German army in Belgium, was doing what he could for five injured soldiers sheltering in a dilapidated hut near a small town called Inden. Suddenly the shed took a direct hit from the artillery of the advancing American forces.

Gretchen Schiller's world fell apart when she received a parcel containing Hans's paybook, identity disc, wallet, wristwatch and the New Testament which was never far from his side. Her son was dead.

She was inconsolable. Her husband had died at the front in 1941 and Hans was her much loved, only child.

Sometime after the war ended she met an old comrade of Hans's who had just been released from a prisoner of war camp. Suddenly there was a glimmer of light in the darkness that had shrouded Gretchen Schiller's world since she had opened that parcel. Hans, the old soldier said, had not died in the allied advance. He had been in an explosion and taken to a field hospital where his terrible head injuries had been treated by an American surgeon. When he was well enough to travel he had been sent to a prisoner of war camp in Britain. He knew this because he had met him there.

Gretchen Schiller knew what she had to do. If her son was alive the only reason he had not come home by now must be that he had lost his memory in the explosion. But if he had not been killed why had she been sent his personal effects? That must have been a mistake. After all, she had never been informed of his place of burial. And with no memory and no papers or identity disc, no one would know who he was. It was up to her to find him.

She wrote direct to the British Red Cross asking for their help. Yvonne Watts, a volunteer in London, contacted the Prisoner of War Information Bureau in Northumberland Avenue. The reply came in four days. It was short and to the point. They had no one

61

called Hans Schiller in their records. Mrs Watts then got in touch with the Bureau's European Head-quarters in case Hans had been held in one of the temporary camps that had been set up behind allied lines as they advanced towards Germany. She also sent an enquiry to the Red Cross Central Tracing Agency in Geneva.

Again there was no record of a Hans Schiller, but there was an unknown soldier who had died in a Belgian hospital on Christmas Eve 1945. He appeared to have been a medical orderly of about Hans's age, weight and height, and his wounds matched those Gretchen had described in her letter to the Red Cross. He had been buried in a grave marked 'Unknown German Soldier' in a peaceful church-yard not far from the hospital.

The Red Cross were certain that the unknown German soldier must be Hans Schiller. Gretchen Schiller refused to accept the information. She knew her son was still alive, and she would find him however long it took.

Gretchen lost count of the number of letters she wrote establishing to which camps soldiers who had been taken prisoner in south Belgium at the end of 1944 had been sent. When she had narrowed it down to half a dozen or so, she set about the awesome task of contacting as many of their former inmates as she could.

None of those who bothered to answer the first batch of letters could help. She wrote again to those who had taken the trouble of replying to her, asking for the names of other soldiers who had been in the camps, and eventually her dogged perseverance paid off. She received a letter from someone who thought he remembered her son. Then another. Then more.

Despite the cost, she had copies made of the photograph from Hans's paybook, now one of her most treasured possessions, and sent them to the men who thought they had known him. Several of those who received the photograph had been held at the Urebank Camp, near Ripon in Yorkshire, and although none of them was one hundred per cent certain that the man in the photograph had been in the camp, two or three thought he might have been.

To Gretchen an uncertain maybe was infinitely better than a definite no. The maybe became a positive yes. She wrote to the Red Cross again giving them the names and numbers of the men from Urebank. Surely, she thought as she waited for the reply, surely the Red Cross would be able to trace Hans now.

The news she received from the Red Cross was not encouraging. The Information Bureau confirmed that the men Gretchen had mentioned had been held in Urebank Camp. But there was still no record of Hans Schiller being a prisoner in that or any other camp.

A woman less determined than Gretchen would have given up. But she knew that as he had no papers, it would be almost impossible for the British to identify her son, with his shell-shattered memory.

Deep in her heart she knew he was still alive and she had to find him.

She wrote to anyone who she thought might help her, no matter how remote the connection: the Yorkshire police, hospitals, nursing homes, she wrote to them all, willing herself to carry on even though the odds were so heavily stacked against her. Most of these enquiries were sent on to the British Red Cross who explained that all avenues of search had been examined and that Gretchen had been given all the available information.

On the day she heard from not one, but two German ex-POWs who said they had worked alongside Hans, she fell to her knees to thank God. Hans had, the men wrote, played the piano at concert parties German POWs staged for people who lived near the camp. It was after the war, a time when German POWs were allowed to mix, under supervision, with people in and around their prisons. For many Germans the rules of war were replaced by the rules of courtship. After one concert Hans, Gretchen was told, had met an attractive redhead and when he had been released, he had decided to stay in England and marry his Titian-haired girlfriend.

A wife! It was a new lead. The thought of asking for marriage records to be checked had never crossed Gretchen's mind. Once again her pen was busy as she contacted town halls and registrars' offices all over Yorkshire. And once again there was no trace of Hans Schiller.

Gretchen would not give up. She paid for posters to be printed and arranged for them to be put up in and around Ripon. Who knows how many people saw Hans's face staring at them from shop windows and parish council noticeboards as they read Gretchen's plea?

Ladies and Gentlemen,
  I am seeking my missing son and my

daughter-in-law. Is there anybody who ever saw my son and my daughter-in-law?

This was followed by as much information about Hans as she could cram onto a small poster; and what she knew about his wife, his love of music and his life in England. Her descriptive details grew with her determination to find him, and with suggestions from people who thought they might have met him.

A barber remembered cutting Hans's hair. Some farm workers recalled working alongside him. Several people wrote that he had played the piano at concert parties, and others that he had been the organist at their local churches.

Gretchen followed up every lead. The police actually interviewed the two men who had told her about Hans's marriage. One of them eventually said he had mistaken Hans for someone else. The other said he knew where the couple lived. But when the police checked, the man had been half right and half wrong. The woman was indeed the redhead he had remembered, but the man she had married was not Hans Schiller, although, to be fair, he had been a German POW and had blue eyes and blond hair.

Still Gretchen refused to give up. In 1965, by which time she thought she had traced her son to a Norfolk asylum and then a market garden in Sussex, her story appeared in the *Baptist Times*.

Many of those who read the report contacted the Red Cross in London. Each call was patiently listened to, each letter carefully read, and each given the same reply. The Red Cross had done everything it possibly could to help trace Hans Schiller. They had enormous sympathy with his mother and had tried to help her to come to terms with the sad, and to them incontrovertible, fact that Hans Schiller was the unknown German soldier who lay in a quiet corner in a churchyard near the hospital where he had died in 1944.

Gretchen's resolve to find her son never wavered. She went on writing her letters to Britain, absolutely sure that one of them would lead to Hans. The last we know of her is in 1972 when she wrote to the Women's Institute. Her pleas was so poignant that several branches circulated the story in their news-letter. But again it proved fruitless.

Every mother, especially those who have had no body over which to grieve, no grave to mourn, will sympathise with Gretchen Schiller. But there comes a time when the door must be closed on the past. If she was right and Hans had survived the war, he would be well into his seventies by now. To Gretchen Schiller he was for ever the studious young man who stared up at her every time she looked lovingly at his photograph, wed to an English girl and still playing the church organ in a small, unknown English village.

The Man with no Name

The Central Tracing Agency's criterion for taking up a search is a simple one: the relatives have 'disappeared' during an armed conflict, a period of civil unrest or violence. Joanna Van Danziger's case met this criterion. She had last seen her son a few months before the Second World War came to an end. So when, in 1977, she asked the Red Cross to try to find him, they had no hesitation in taking on the case. She had borne him because of the war, and she had then lost him because of the war . . .

Joanna Van Boven was fifteen when German soldiers occupied Holland. Joanna's family life revolved around a staunch Protestant faith which frowned upon frivolity and demanded a strict upbringing for children. Her mother was a forceful woman; her father a strong disciplinarian.

When Joanna was nineteen, she fell in love with a handsome young German soldier, Hans Nillson. They had to meet in secret, for not only did Joanna know that her father would move heaven and earth to stop the affair, but girls who fraternized with the enemy were ostracised and sometimes assaulted by other women.

In February 1944, Joanna was horrified when she realized that she was three months pregnant. It was Hans's baby, but by now he had already been posted to France. She behaved as many other women in her situation do: she tried to carry on as if nothing was wrong – and prayed for a miracle!

Her prayers went unanswered, and knowing she couldn't hide her condition any longer, she forced herself to face the awful truth and confront her parents.

'There is no place for you here any longer. There never will be again,' was her father's cold response.

As Joanna packed what clothes she could cram into her small holdall, she thought her world had come to an end. Her lover was hundreds of miles away. Her parents had cut her out of their lives. She knew that no one in the suburban little town would take pity on her. She took her heavy coat off its hanger. It was winter: she would need it.

She cut a forlorn figure as she walked slowly down the stairs, holdall in one hand, handbag in the other, the thick, woollen coat draped around her shoulders. The door to the parlour was firmly closed. Her father would be in his chair to the right of the stove; her mother in hers on the left; the chair opposite the stove, her chair, empty. She made no move to go into the room. There would be no change of heart. No farewell embrace. Not even a 'God go with you.' Joanna Van Boven went down the hall, opened the front door and walked out of her parents' lives.

She made her way to Amsterdam and even now is reluctant to talk about her experiences until, on 21 August, she gave birth to a baby boy whom she called Erwin. There had been no word from Hans for weeks. She read about the heavy German casualties after the D-Day landings in Normandy and knew in her heart that he was dead. Cut off from her family, she was, apart from her little baby, quite alone in the world.

Holland held nothing for her so she decided to go to Germany to try to build a new life. But with the Third Reich crumbling all around and the sniff of defeat in the air, there was nothing for her there either, so for the third time in her life she turned her back on the past. She packed her meagre possessions into her shabby holdall, tucked her baby into a carry cot and set off for Prague.

If things were bad in Germany, they were even worse in Czechoslovakia. There were no jobs, no food and with no savings to fall back on, Joanna could scarcely look after herself, let alone little Erwin. She had no idea where to turn until, praying that she was doing the right thing, she gave her baby into the care of the Red Cross.

When the war came to an end, things began to look up for Joanna. She went back to Holland where she married and settled down. She often wondered what had happened to Erwin. How was he growing up? What did he look like? Was he doing well at school, and later, what was he doing for a living? The feeling that she would like to see him again grew into an aching need that deepened with each year that passed. In 1977 she knew she had to try to find him.

The Red Cross agreed to help. Their records showed that after Joanna had handed Erwin over to them, he had been cared for in a home and then fostered with a Czech family. They traced him to Austria where they were told he had emigrated to Britain in 1975. When the enquiry was pursued by the British Red Cross they traced someone whose personal details indicated he could well be Erwin.

The letter they wrote to him outlined the details that Joanna had given the International Red Cross Tracing Service, and contained the usual assurance that she would only be given Erwin's address if he agreed. 'If you are not the person concerned,' they wrote, 'we are sorry to have troubled you.'

It took two months for Erwin to reply that he was sure that he was Joanna's son and asking the Red Cross to give his mother his address. Joanna was overjoyed when she received the news, and a few weeks later, she was in London to see the son she had given to the Red Cross in the final days of the war. Her stomach churned as she walked across the lobby of London's Hilton Hotel. As she approached him, she held out her hand as if to shake his. 'Erwin?' she murmured.

'Mama!' the handsome, well-dressed man sighed, and ignoring her hand he engulfed her in his arms. If Joanna had any fears that Erwin would be bitter about being abandoned, they evaporated in that embrace.

Later, over dinner, Erwin told his mother that when he had finished school in Prague, he had enrolled in an Austrian catering college. In 1975 he had come to England to work as a waiter at the Hilton. She listened with growing pride when he said that he had been quickly promoted to head barman and then purchasing manager before leaving to set himself up as an art dealer.

The week that Joanna spent in London with Erwin was one of the happiest of her life. She left, weighed down with gifts, promising to keep in touch with him and over the next ten years they wrote to each other regularly and Joanna came to London several times to see her son, or the man she thought was her son.

In 1988, the British Red Cross were surprised when they received another enquiry about Erwin Van Boven. This time from the police. The officers who called at Grosvenor Crescent in London were told that according to Red Cross rules of confidentiality no information could be divulged without the permission of the person concerned or his next of kin and that information concerning tracing enquiries could only be used for humanitarian reasons.

'We don't want to trace him,' came the reply. 'We know where he is. In our cells, detained on serious charges.'

While the Red Cross were not able to give the police the information they had without a legal requirement to do so, they were able to discuss what other channels might be used to obtain details of the person concerned.

Joanna was heart-broken when she learned that the handsome, charming man she thought was her son was in fact a fraud, a spy with a mission to gather top-secret information about Polaris and other aspects of British defence policy from the agents he recruited, and pass it on to Prague.

A few months later, Erwin Van Boven stood in the dock at the Old Bailey. His trial lasted for five days during which it emerged that the real Erwin had died of meningitis when he was seven. Years later, when the Czechs wanted to establish a false identity for one of their agents, they went through the records to find someone born about the same time but who had died in childhood. They came up with Erwin Van Boven. He was given a Czech passport in Erwin's name, and after intense training he was sent to catering school in Austria. There, he wrote to Queen Juliana of the Netherlands claiming to be a displaced Dutch citizen and was given a Dutch passport.

From Austria, he went to London and the Hilton.

After a year or two, he left his job at the five-star hotel announcing that he was setting himself up as an art dealer. He then enrolled for art classes to pick up the jargon of the trade.

As well as sending British defence secrets to Prague, the debonair spy also infiltrated British groups that supported Jewish dissidents in eastern Europe. He even acted as interpreter when they visited Moscow and posed for souvenir photographs with the very men and women he later betrayed to his Soviet paymasters.

In 1985, Vlasimil Lubvik, a Czech diplomat, defected to the West. Among the names of Czech agents working in Britain he gave to MI5 was Erwin Van Boven. The British kept him under surveillance for eighteen months, during which time the unsuspecting agent continued to run his spy network.

He was caught red-handed in 1988 when police broke into his North London flat, and found him crouched over a radio taking a message from Prague. When he was arrested, he asked only that the Czech embassy in London be notified of his arrest.

A police search of the scruffy little apartment turned up a spy kit that could have come straight from the pages of *Boy's Own* magazine. There was a powerful, portable two-way radio, a hollowed-out bar of soap and a tin of pain-killers both of which contained secret codes, a pile of glossy women's magazines and his two passports.

'Van Boven', it transpired, received instructions from his Prague controllers in Morse code via the radio. When he had gathered the information they wanted, he used invisible ink to write coded messages in the fashion magazines which he posted to Czechoslovakia.

He refused to defend himself during his five-day trial and also refused to reveal his true identity. He showed no emotion when the judge said to him, 'I address you as Erwin Van Boven, although I am convinced it was not your name at birth.

'You are a dedicated, resourceful spy. If you had not been caught, you would have done whatever your Czech controllers told you to do, however hurtful that might have been to this country's interest.

'It is necessary to most jealously guard the freedom of this nation.'

Back in Holland, Joanna blinked away her tears as she read that the man who had embraced her and called her 'Mama' had taken the secret of his true identity with him to the cells.

It was as if she had lost her son twice over. The British Red Cross had done their best to assist Joanna. They would, of course, have much preferred him to write 'I am not the person concerned' and then no further action would have been taken and the two would never have met.

Hands Across the Ocean

The smaller of the two men sitting in the Red Cross office had been ill. His skin was grey and fell from his face in deep folds. When he spoke, it was through a rasping breath.

His friend was a picture of health. Strong featured, sturdily built and with the sort of ruddy glow that comes from spending long hours in the open air.

'Now. How can we help?' Ann Scott's voice was warm and friendly.

'This is my friend, Jan,' said the larger man, in the perfectly rounded tones of rural Sussex. 'He's been in hospital.' He laid his hand on the middle of his chest to emphasise the point. 'Heart trouble.

'He's staying with my wife and me till he gets better. On our farm. Near Cuckfield.'

'And what can the Red Cross do for you?' Ann smiled at Jan as she spoke . . .

In 1945, just before the German surrender, Jan Slowacki, like thousands of other innocent civilians, found himself trapped in the remnants of German-held territory, with Russian troops storming towards Berlin from the east and British and American infantry advancing through the Rhineland from the west.

When the war in Europe came to an end, Jan was sent to a displaced persons' camp where he made friends with Uta Bulganin, an attractive young woman from the Ukraine. As the months passed they became lovers. Many people were making plans for a new life in a new country, but Uta was dreading the future. She literally shook with fear when she told Jan that many people were being forced to return to the Soviet Union. 'I can't go back there,' she wept. 'There is nothing for me. Nothing!' But she was helpless.

Jan's heart went out to the distraught woman. 'She can't go back,' he said to himself. 'She can't.' And when, a few months later, he was offered a chance to start a new life in England, he asked, 'May I bring my wife with me? She is here in the camp.'

Few of the refugees had any documentation let alone marriage certificates. The British officer nodded before wearily stamping a piece of paper and scribbling 'and wife' alongside Jan's name.

Jan sprinted back to his hut to break the news to Uta. 'But we're not married,' she gasped.

'Don't worry about that,' Jan reassured her. 'We'll think of something.' And sure enough, a few hours later, Jan and Uta knelt before a makeshift altar, reciting the marriage vows in the presence of a refugee Polish priest.

The camps were an administrative nightmare and it was some months before Uta and Jan arrived in Britain, where they were sent to a refugee camp in Hampshire. Their room contained a bed and a few sticks of furniture. But it was a room of their own. And if they had to share a kitchen and bathroom with other new arrivals, no one cared.

Uta knew that Jan cared for her more than she did for him. But she was so grateful for what he had done, that she did her best to make their marriage work. Two years after they arrived in Britain, she gave birth to a son whom they called Waslaw. Things were starting to go well for Jan. He had a wife, and now he had a son. For the first time since 1939, he had a future worth planning for.

His happiness was short lived. Waslaw was a few weeks old when Uta told Jan that she had met again and was in love with Andrei Shakhin, another Ukrainian refugee she had previously known in the camp. 'I didn't want to. I tried not to,' she wept.

Jan's world fell apart. He had always known that Uta did not love him. She was grateful: he knew that. But she did not love him. He had hoped that maybe one day . . .

'I want a divorce,' Uta said when Jan had recovered a little.

'I cannot hold you against your will, but what will happen to Waslaw?' Jan asked.

'A baby's place is with his mother.' Uta's words cut through Jan's heart, but he knew that she was right. Shortly after the divorce, Uta married the man she truly loved, and Jan agreed that his son should be legally adopted by the couple. Almost as soon as the formalities had been completed, Uta, her new husband, and her – now their – child set sail for a new life in Canada.

As the years passed, Jan made many friends who introduced him to lots of attractive women, but none of them fuelled the same feelings in him as Uta had, and he never married again. He devoted himself to his business, driving himself harder and harder until, one day in the early 1970s, he collapsed with a massive heart attack.

As he lay in his hospital bed, his thoughts drifted back over the years. He had naturally often wondered how life had treated Uta and Waslaw, but he had never tried to get in touch with them, that wouldn't have been fair. But now, with death knocking at his door, he felt he had to find them again.

When Jan was discharged from hospital, one of his friends asked him to convalesce on his Sussex farm, an invitation that was gratefully accepted. Although the elderly Pole made a good recovery, the kindly farmer often found him staring wistfully into space. At first he put this down to the heart attack, but one evening when Jan had been sitting on the terrace, lost in a world of his own, he suddenly said, 'I need to see my son. I need to see Waslaw.'

'And that's why you're here?' Ann Scott looked at Jan as she spoke very slowly. 'You want us to find Waslaw?'

Jan nodded. 'Waslaw.' He repeated the name softly. 'I would like you to find my Waslaw.'

Ann explained that after a gap of over twenty-five years, tracing Jan's ex-wife and son could take some time, if it could be done at all.

As soon the two men had left her office, she got in touch with the British Red Cross Tracing Service in London. She would, she wrote, be grateful if the case could be given priority. Jan was obviously very weak. If he had another heart attack, it could well prove fatal. The British Red Cross contacted their Canadian colleagues immediately.

It didn't take too long for the Canadian Red Cross to establish the province in which Uta and her husband were believed to have settled. Within weeks of the request being received Anne-Marie Dupont, a French-Canadian Red Cross volunteer, was on the telephone to a Uta Shakhin who, she was quite certain, was the woman she was looking for.

Yes, Uta guardedly confirmed, she had once been married to Jan Slowacki. And yes, she went on, she had a son called Waslaw. Why did the Red Cross want to know? And now, after such a long period?

When Anne-Marie told Uta about Jan's failing health and his desire to find his son was explained to her, the line went quiet.

'Are you still there?' asked Mlle Dupont.

There was no response.

'Does Waslaw live with you?'

'No, he got married last year.' Anne-Marie could almost hear the suspicion flow down the line. 'Candy and he live not far from here.' Uta's voice was still strained. 'I'm sorry . . . You see . . . I've never told Waslaw he was adopted. He thinks Andrei is his real father . . .'

'Would you like to think about it and call me back?' said Anne-Marie and gave Uta her number. No sooner had she finished than there was a click and the line went dead.

All Anne-Marie could do now was wait. The very next day Uta was on the phone.

'I owe everything to Jan,' she said. 'If it hadn't been for him, I would have been sent back to the

Ukraine in 1945 and who knows what would have happened. So, yes, I will tell you where Waslaw is.'

'Thank you,' said Anne-Marie. 'Thank you so much.'

'There is just one thing,' Uta paused. 'Could you wait a day or two before you contact him? He'll need to know the truth. It'll be such a shock, you see. It's all very complicated. He's always wanted to become a Canadian citizen, but without a birth certificate . . .'

'What happened to it?' Anne-Marie was puzzled. 'Surely you brought it with you . . .'

'No. I was scared he would find it and see that Andrei was not his real father. So I . . .' Her voice faded before she continued. 'He has his baptismal certificate. But the Canadians still won't give him citizenship.'

When Uta broke the news to Waslaw, his first reaction was disbelief. Then he felt hurt. Then betrayed. 'Why didn't you tell me?' The pain in his voice was heart-breaking.

'There was no need at first,' Uta wept as she spoke. 'We always meant to but kept putting it off. And then it was too late. Too late . . .' she repeated. 'And without a birth certificate, there was no need.'

It took some time for Waslaw to calm down, but the more he thought about it the more he came to understand what his mother had been through and the sacrifice that Jan had made. By the time Anne-Marie Dupont contacted him to find out if he would agree for his name to be given to Jan Slowacki, his mind was made up.

It was in December 1974, just two months after Jan and his friend had gone into the Red Cross Branch office in Sussex, that the old Pole was told that his son was alive and that he had just got married. Jan beamed when he heard he had a daughter-in-law.

'Can he come and see me?' he asked, his eyes glittering with tears. 'And his wife? I have enough to pay their fares.'

'Would you and your wife like to fly to England to meet your father?' Anne-Marie asked, back in Canada. 'He said he would pay for you both to fly to England! It sounds perfect.' And then, seeing Waslaw's face cloud, she asked. 'Is something the matter?'

'I can't go to England. I haven't got a passport,' Waslaw said.

'Let's see what we can arrange, shall we?'

Anne-Marie advised Waslaw to apply for a travel document, something which is usually only issued to refugees who have lost their identification papers or passports when they fled to freedom.

While all this was going on, back in England Jan was becoming increasingly agitated. Ann Scott, knowing the precarious state of Jan's health, was at her most persuasive when she talked him out of flying to Canada himself. 'Only a few more days,' she said. 'And you'll see your son.'

In early March 1975, an Air Canada jumbo jet with Waslaw and Candice Shakhin on board landed at Heathrow where a Red Cross volunteer was waiting to whisk them to Sussex. As the car sped along the country lanes, Waslaw said very little. Candy squeezed his hand. 'Don't worry,' she whispered.

80

'What am I going to say to him? What if we don't like each other? What if . . .' his voice faded.

'Don't worry,' she said again. 'It'll be all right.'

Jan had never really mastered English, and Waslaw knew only a little Polish and had a smattering of Ukrainian, both of which sounded very odd when spoken in a soft Canadian drawl, but it wasn't long before the barriers were broken and the frail sixty-year-old father and his rather serious twenty-seven-year-old son were getting on famously.

The young couple spent as much time with Jan as possible, but he insisted that they went to London where Waslaw was able to get a copy of his birth certificate from Somerset House. All the way back on the train to Sussex, he kept tapping the pocket in which it nestled, reassuring himself that it was still there. At last, he could apply for Canadian citizenship.

When Jan saw his own name written in the registrar's elegant, copper-plate script in the column headed 'Father' his eyes filled with tears of pride.

In her notes about the case, Ann Scott wrote, 'Without the Red Cross, Waslaw would never have known about his true father's existence. He would never have come to England. The Red Cross brought them together and ensured that a fine old man did not spend his last days with no one to call his own.'

Look at the Stars and feel Glad

During the Uprising of 1956, thousands of Hungarians fled to Austria. And in the immediate aftermath of the revolution that followed, wave upon wave of battle-bruised men, women and children flocked across the border, fleeing from a government even more intolerant of opposition than the one it had replaced.

The refugees were emotionally shell-shocked. One of them still recalls how his distraught wife knotted a handful of Hungarian soil into a tear-stained handkerchief and vowed to keep it with her until the day it would be safe for her to come home.

Some Hungarians, wary of an uncertain future in a foreign land, decided to stay where they were, but sent their children to safety. A woman who worked for the Red Cross at the time remembers a group of bemused boys and girls turning up at the border with labels around their necks pleading: 'Look after our children; we stay behind to fight.'

Life in the makeshift camps was grim. It was mid-winter and temperatures were sub-zero. Water froze in the pipes. Food was scarce. Conditions were primitive. The Red Cross and other international agencies struggled to do what they could to assist the refugees, many of whom had left their children with relatives in Hungary, rather than risk their lives in the exhausting trek to the border.

But if it could do nothing to influence events in eastern Europe, at least the West could offer some sort of home, some sort of hope to the homeless and now stateless Hungarians. Slowly, the makeshift camps in Austria emptied as the Hungarian refugees were resettled around Europe, Australia, North America and other countries.

Among those who were offered a new life in Britain were Janos and Julia Rajk. They had fled from Barbacs, the tiny village where they had been born, leaving their three young children to be looked after by relatives. Julia had been heart-broken as she kissed Ferenc, little Janos and Dora goodbye, but her husband had reassured her that it wouldn't be for long. And as soon as they had been housed and Janos had found a job, they began to make arrangements for the children to join them.

The Hungarian authorities, however, had other ideas. Janos lost count of the number of letters he wrote to Budapest, begging that their children be given exit visas. The few that were answered all carried the same, devastating decision, No!

Slowly, the unthinkable became the unbearable. Unless things changed, they would never see their children again.

As time passed, Janos and Julia tried to put the past behind them and pick up the pieces of their shattered lives. They moved to Lancashire and, even though they had four more children, they never gave up their cherished hope of eventually being reunited with the three they had left behind in Hungary.

In 1962, six years after the Hungarian Revolution, Janos heard about the Red Cross Tracing Service.

He immediately wrote to the Central Tracing Agency in Geneva asking if anything could be done to get his children out of Hungary. The enquiry was forwarded to the British Red Cross and the Hungarian Red Cross.

The Hungarian Red Cross eventually tracked down the three Rajk children, but by the time they got the information to Britain, circumstances had changed dramatically. Julia Rajk had been diagnosed as having tuberculosis. Janos had slumped into a severe depression and, unable to face the prospect of life without his childhood sweetheart, had killed himself.

Despite her numbing grief and increasing frailty, Julia forced herself to make plans for the future. After weeks of agonising, she decided that it would be best for all the family if she took her four British-born children to Hungary. She somehow found the stamina to battle with the bureaucracy at the Hungarian embassy in London, and eventually persuaded them to issue the necessary papers.

But just two days before she and her children were due to set off for Hungary, and exactly a year to the day after Janos had committed suicide, Julia died.

As she lay on her deathbed, she whispered to her children's Hungarian godmother that she wanted her children to go to Hungary as she had planned. But Anna, Julia, Sofia and Tamas Rajk were sent to a Catholic children's home while social workers pondered their future. The Church, claiming that the children would not be free to practise catholicism in communist Hungary, argued that they should stay in Britain.

Julia's relatives, backed by the Hungarian government, begged the British authorities to allow the children to go to them.

The British prevaricated. The Hungarian Ministry for Foreign Affairs complained through the state-owned press that Britain was denying a Hungarian woman her dying wish that her children be allowed to settle in Hungary.

Section 17 of the 1948 Children's Act empowered the British Home Office to allow orphaned children to leave the country to live with relatives overseas, only if it was satisfied that the children would benefit, and that suitable arrangements had been or would be made for the children's reception and welfare in their new country.

Whitehall, not convinced that these conditions would be met, did not urge that the Rajk children should leave the country. The Red Cross had no power to influence events, and so they had to abandon the case. However the British Red Cross kept the file, and so all the details were retained. Julia and Janos Rajk's seven children remain grateful for that policy to this day.

Anna, Julia, Sofia and Tamas Rajk were lucky. They were kept together and fostered by a family in Derbyshire who gave them a stable background and a very happy childhood. As time passed, memories of their parents grew dimmer.

When Anna, the youngest of the four, was eight, Alice Marks, her foster-mother, thought the time had come to tell the children what she knew about their past. They listened intently as they learned that their real parents had been Hungarians, that their father had died exactly a year before their mother, and that it had been thought best that the children be fostered, rather than be sent to Hungary to be brought up by relatives there.

That was all that Alice knew and, although the youngsters were naturally curious, they didn't badger her for more information in case they upset her.

But as Anna said many years later, 'Even then, I longed to find out about my roots.'

When Anna was eighteen, the fostering agency gave the Rajks access to their case histories. The files contained the scantiest of information – little more than their names, reports from the home they had been sent to, Julia's last address and some dates.

As Anna read the notes in her file, she felt a great surge of emotion well up inside her and she determined to find out as much as she could about her mother and father.

The first thing she wanted to do was to visit their graves. It took months of research before she found out where her parents had been buried. Lesser souls would have given up, but Anna was like a dog with a bone. She would not rest until she had put flowers on her parents' graves.

As it turned out, there had been no money for proper funerals, and it was a heartbroken young woman who knelt by the paupers' grave where Janos and Julia had been buried along with sixteen others. Her prayers were said in a soft whisper as she tearfully placed flowers on the spot where her parents lay.

Anna was devastated but she was still determined to find out as much about her parents as she could. By pure chance, the Rajks heard that a Hungarian

REUNITED!

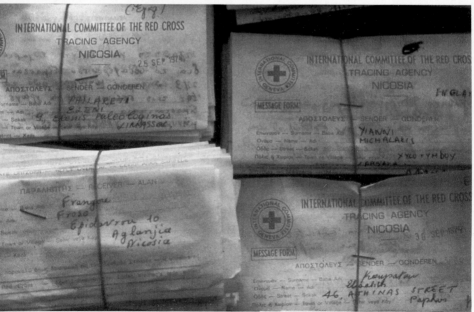

Top: The longest telegram ever received by the Central Tracing Agency: 2,341 names of prisoners of war (ICRC)

Above: Red Cross Message forms for Cyprus (ICRC)

Top: Iran–Iraq War: wounded Iranian POWs repatriated by ICRC (ICRC)
Above: Iran–Iraq War: ICRC delegate registering Iranian POWs (ICRC)

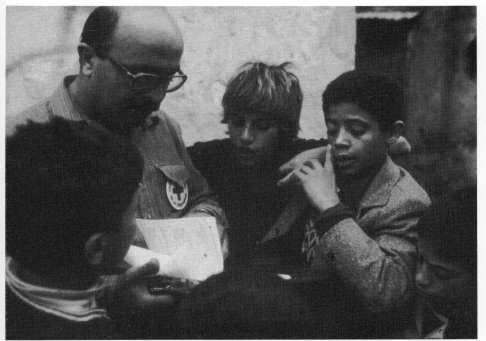

Top: Lebanon: distributing messages in the street (ICRC)
Above: Lebanon: writing and translating messages in the street (ICRC)

Reunited! Clockwise from above left: In Hungary: 'Look at the Stars and Feel Glad'; brother and sister at the Berlin Wall after forty years apart; a Bosnian family; grandmother and grandsons in Zagreb, Croatia; two sisters and their brother who survived concentration camps, with their Red Cross case worker (Mail on Sunday, Network, Dick Harding, ICRC, Okello Albino)

Top: ICRC delegate in Africa involved in tracing activities (BRCS)
Above: Sierra Leone; tracing board with lists of names (ICRC)

Top: Rwanda; unaccompanied children – Nyashe being registered (ICRC)

Above: Rwanda; unaccompanied children – the Red Cross worker is looking for distinguishing marks (ICRC)

Top: Records at the Central Tracing Agency in Geneva (ICRC)

Above: Lady Limerick, Chairman of the British Red Cross, and Sandra Singer with Charles Biedermann, the Director of the International Tracing Service in Arolsen, Germany (ITS)

woman called Maria Nagy, who may have been their godmother, was still alive and living in Lancashire. Anna wrote to her.

The days dragged by. Anna was beside herself with nerves. What would happen if the Maria Nagy she had written to was not, after all, the Maria Nagy who was her godmother? And if she was, perhaps she had died before she received the letter. Worse! What if the Maria Nagy she had written to was her godmother, but refused for some reason or other to see her?

Her heart leapt when one morning, among the bills, letters and circulars, the postman delivered an envelope written in a hand she did not recognize. Anna ripped it open and began to read the letter with difficulty, partly because it was written in very spidery handwriting, and partly because her eyes misted over with tears as she read that, yes, the writer was the Maria Nagy who had known Julia Rajk, and, yes, Julia had asked her to be godmother to her children. Of course, she would be overjoyed to see her godchildren again, though she doubted she would recognize them after so many years. But why didn't Anna phone and arrange a date to come and see her?

How wonderful, thought Anna, it was going to be to talk to someone who had actually known her mother and father. But as the day drew nearer, she became anxious. What if Maria's memory was not what it had been? What if she found it painful to talk about the past?

Her fears were soon dispelled. The old lady was bright as a button and was soon chuckling as she regaled Anna with stories about Janos and Julia.

Julia had been a great cook whose kitchen was always full of delicious smells. And Janos had liked nothing better than filling his house with friends and neighbours.

Then Maria's voice saddened and Anna gulped hard to keep her tears at bay as she heard how Julia had become paler and thinner as tuberculosis took its terrible toll, and how, as his wife grew weaker and weaker, Janos had become so depressed that he had killed himself.

Anna could not stop herself crying when Maria told her about the night she had held Julia's hand and listened to the whispered dying wish that all her children be united in Hungary.

All her children! None of the British-born Rajks had known of the existence of their brothers and sister. As Maria talked, Anna was pre-occupied with the thought of breaking this wonderful news to Julia, Sofia and Tamas.

Knowing that their mother had died desperate for her family to be together, the Rajks decided to track down the brothers and sister they had never met, whose very existence they had been unaware of for most of their lives.

But where should they start? They couldn't even find Barbacs, their parents' village, on a large-scale map of Hungary. Then, early in 1989, a friend told Anna about the British Red Cross Tracing Service.

By an extraordinary coincidence, the Hungarian Rajks, increasingly curious about their English brother and sisters, had already asked the Hungarian Red Cross to try to trace them.

It turned out to be one of the least difficult tracing

jobs the Tracing Service has been asked to undertake, because the British Red Cross already had all
the details on file for just such an eventuality. And
when the Hungarian Red Cross tracing request was
received in London, it didn't take long to trace
Anna's sister, Julia, through her centralised records.

And so it was that one day in 1989, a member of
the Red Cross contacted Julia and, with the tact that
comes with years of experience, told her that Janos
Rajk had asked the Hungarian Red Cross to trace his
British-born brother and sisters. She explained to the
dumbstruck Julia that any information about them
could only be passed to Janos if Julia and the others
agreed.

Anna was overjoyed. 'It meant so much to know
that Janos had cared about us all this time,' she said.

As soon as they had Janos's address, Anna and
Julia wrote to him. The English Rajks spoke no
Magyar. The Hungarian Rajks had a smattering of
English. But that didn't stop both families ex-
changing a stream of postcards and letters, and
countless photographs.

Everyone was desperate to know everything about
everyone else – what they looked like, what they did
for a living, whether or not they were married, if they
had children . . . No detail was too small.

It wasn't long before letters, no matter how lively
and loving, and photographs, no matter how clear
and colourful, proved unsatisfactory. They had to
meet.

The Hungarian Red Cross helped with the
arrangements and, in October 1989, a car carrying
Anna, Julia, Sofia and Tamas drove into Barbacs,
their parents' birthplace. The car came to a halt in

the fading evening light outside a small hotel.

Anna tried to stifle the nagging doubt she had that perhaps the two families would not get on. Her stomach churning, she got out first and came face to face with someone she was sure she recognized. Seconds later, she was hugging the sister, Dora, she had never met before. There were hugs and tears as the seven made their way to Janos's house, the house their parents had left in 1956.

Later that night, as Anna, Julia, Sofia and Tamas lay in their beds, their heads still spinning from the events of the day, they could hardly believe that, after being separated for so long, all that stood between them and their Hungarian family now were thin bedroom walls.

The Red Cross had arranged for interpreters to be on hand, but the newly united family found they could communicate almost without language; it seemed as if they had known each other all their lives.

The week flashed by. There were tears, there was laughter, there were hugs. Anna was so happy she kept pinching herself to make sure she wasn't dreaming.

She still does. The seven are in constant touch with each other and whenever Anna misses Janos, Dora and Ferenc she thinks of what Dora said to her as they hugged each other goodbye: 'Don't cry,' she sobbed. 'Look at the stars at night and feel glad – we'll be looking at the same stars, thinking of you.'

I Think About Them Every Day . . .

As the North Vietnamese intensified their military activities in South Vietnam, over three million western servicemen and women, mostly American, were despatched to the area in a long but futile campaign to keep the country 'free'.

The world switched on its television sets to witness some of the most distressing scenes ever filmed: Vietnamese of both sides pressing their revolvers against the temples of captured enemies; depersonalized US prisoners of war repeating the mantra of the inevitability of a communist victory; young girls selling their bodies to American GIs on the street corners of Saigon; soldiers storming through the jungle with guns and flame throwers; American aircraft carpet bombing northern cities and spraying vast areas of jungle with napalm and other defoliants hoping to flush out Viet Cong guerillas.

Equally shocking were the pathetic pictures of teenage mothers huddled hopelessly in alleyways, cradling their half-American babies in their skinny arms. But most horrifying of all was the picture seen world-wide of children running towards the cameras, the flesh burning on their bodies.

These pictures imprinted themselves on the world's consciousness. Then, in the last days of the conflict, when the North Vietnamese were tightening their grip on the South and it became clear that Saigon would fall, rumours were rife that children too would be victimised by the North Vietnamese and would not be safe. This led some well-intentioned charities, who were already working with children, to feel they had to evacuate them; which, in turn, led to mothers handing over their children to orphanages.

The Red Cross did not get involved in this. Not because they didn't feel for the youngsters of Vietnam. Of course they did: as in almost every conflict for over 130 years, there were Red Cross workers in the field doing whatever they could for all victims of the war. However, there was no evidence that the children were to be killed and, with the wisdom that comes with so many decades of such experience, they suggested that uprooting children and settling them in an alien culture can cause as many problems as it solves.

The airlift sponsored by the readers of Britain's *Daily Mail* left Saigon in April 1975. Among the youngsters who landed in England the next day was ten-year-old Hang.

Hang was typical of thousands of young Vietnamese. Born in 1965 to a girl who was barely in her teens, he never knew his GI father. The baby was brought up by his mother and grandmother who lavished their love on him.

When the little boy was born no one really believed that the North Vietnamese stood any chance against the mighty US war machine. Nine years later, the Americans had withdrawn, the Vietnamese army were retreating further and further south as first one city and then another fell to Ho Chi

Minh's soldiers. The bustling city of Hang's early years fell into a state of panic-stricken anarchy.

His mother was terrified. What would happen to Hang? When she heard that plans were afoot to airlift children out of the country, she begged her parish priest to get him into an orphanage and then find him a place on a flight. And when she was told that Hang was to be one of the lucky ones, she wept with both happiness and despair.

'These people who are taking the children out,' she pleaded, 'must tell him to write. Write to the church – it will be safer.'

When Minh waved goodbye to her son, there was a brave smile on her face, but her heart was breaking. She had no idea when or even if she would see him again.

Hang and the others came off the plane dazed, drowsy and dazzled by the flashes of the countless cameras that greeted them. The children were taken to a large house run by a British charity where the staff begged the journalists and press photographers to leave them in peace.

Offers of assistance poured in from the kind-hearted British public, and from well-intentioned couples keen to adopt a Vietnamese child. When he was asked if he would like British parents, Hang refused. 'My mother is still alive,' he said bravely. 'I don't need two mothers. I already have one.'

After he arrived in England, Hang wrote to his mother, at her church as she had told him to, and sent her a photograph of himself taken in the garden of his new home. He waited and waited for a reply, but as the weeks of silence stretched into months, eager anticipation turned to bitter disappointment.

Reunited!

The charity caring for him did not seem able to help him. They were keen that he should get on with his life. He was bright and he was soon offered a place in a public school paid for by a wealthy sponsor.

Hang worked hard and excelled at his lessons, but the huge cultural difference between himself and his fellow boarders set him apart and he was left much to himself. He sat, and passed, his O levels. Then he left school and enrolled at a sixth-form college to study for A levels.

In 1984, nine years after Hang had arrived in England, a magazine featured him in a 'where-are-they-now' article about the Vietnamese children who had been airlifted to Britain. By this time Hang had passed his A levels with distinction and was about to go to university. When he was asked about his feelings for his mother and his grandmother, he smiled a little and said he missed them. 'I think about them every day and wonder what they may be doing.' However, he had learned to cope, and quickly added, 'I try to forget about it really because I've got my own life to lead and it's best to get on.'

At the British Red Cross office in London, Sandra Singer read the magazine article with interest. She realised that Hang needed to know about his mother, but also that he was trying to concentrate on his life in England and on his studies. She filed the article away thoughtfully.

Hang had no way of knowing that the letter sent to his mother had never been received. After Saigon fell, there was chaos in the city, and the priest to whom Hang had addressed his letter was the only link. He had fled the country.

By pure coincidence, a few months later a letter

written in tortuously fractured English found its way on to Sandra's desk. It had been addressed to the BBC in London, who had sent it to the Central Tracing Agency in Geneva, from where it had been posted back to London.

The letter was from Minh. After she explained what had happened to Hang, she went on:

'Maybe you understand the great love of mothers to their children . . . So I am suffering and I can die if I do not know where he is and how he is now.

'I am hungry to know information of my loving son. I wish to request your humanity and your efficiency with the organisation concerned in order that I may be known information about my son as soon as possible.

'I strongly believe in your humanitarian assistance and your efficiency.

'May God repay the whole of you for what you help me to obtain my desire.'

Because the Red Cross had kept detailed records of all those who had arrived from South East Asia, including the children who had been airlifted out of Vietnam, one of the Tracing Service staff had already attached the basic information held on Hang to the letter. Sandra remembered the article and got it out. And so his question 'I wonder what they may be doing' was so easily answered. Hang was contacted over his mother's letter, and she in turn was given his address.

As far as the Red Cross was concerned, another tracing enquiry had been successfully completed and the papers were filed. They were surprised, therefore, when a few years later they received another enquiry about Hang, this time from the Vietnamese Red Cross who had been approached by Minh, asking them if they could find her son.

When the British Red Cross got in touch with Hang again, he explained that he and his mother had exchanged a few letters, but the correspondence soon fizzled out.

'You can tell her where I am now if you want,' he said indifferently. 'I don't mind either way.'

The Red Cross did not find this reaction surprising! To Hang his mother was a shadowy figure who lived in his dreams, someone who had little to do with his present problems. She was a woman with whom he had had no contact for nearly half his life. He had had to put his life in Vietnam behind him, and he had come to look upon England as his home. His need to find and be with his mother and grandmother had to be put aside – he wanted to find them, but not now.

Hang's case highlights one of the difficulties that arise when children are separated from their parents to be settled in strange lands. It is a frightening and bewildering time for the child and if contact is lost, it is only natural over a period of time that the physical separation affects how the relationship is perceived by the child.

Perhaps if Hang had been offered support and counselling as soon as he had arrived in Britain, and if efforts had been made earlier to trace and to re-establish contact with his mother, it would not have been such a shock for him when she suddenly came back into his life.

I Thank You for Your Prayers

One of the great trouble-spots of the late twentieth century has been the Middle East. First the Arab-Israeli conflict, then inter-Arab wars have wrought havoc in the area almost continually since the Second World War came to an end.

In September 1980, fighter pilot Faisal Al Mahabad was flying his Mirage low over enemy territory when it was hit by a rocket. With the flames licking at his flying boots, Faisal pressed the ejector-seat button; no sooner had he been propelled out of the cockpit, than the fuel tank exploded and the jet crashed into the desert with a display of pyrotechnics that lit up the sky for miles around.

Faisal had no chance of escape. As his parachute landed on the ground, he found himself staring down the barrel of an enemy rifle. Minutes later, regardless of the injuries he sustained, his captors bundled him into the back of a truck. They kept their guns trained on him as the driver rammed the engine into gear and brought his foot down hard on the accelerator. The truck shot forwards and sped across the rock-strewn landscape towards a nearby holding camp, shaking like a roadbuilder's drill as it went.

A few days later, Faisal and several of his fellow prisoners, now all *hors de combat*, were driven to a prisoner of war camp where Faisal was taken to the makeshift hospital wing.

Both sides in the conflict were signatories to the 1949 Geneva Convention whereby they undertook to advise the ICRC of all prisoners taken in time of war. Shortly after his capture, Faisal was registered by a delegate of the ICRC who asked if he wanted to send a family message to anyone. The size of the Red Cross Message form permits only a certain number of words; but enough for Faisal to tell his wife, Sofia, that he was alive and that he loved her and their two infant sons.

A few months later a nervous young man walked into the Red Cross London headquarters.

'Can I help you?' the receptionist asked him.

'My name is Bassim Al Mahabad,' he said softly. 'I want to find out about your Tracing Service.'

It wasn't long before a Red Cross tracing officer was listening sympathetically to Bassim's story. Sofia back home had received two Red Cross Messages from Faisal, but that had been months ago, and she had no idea where he was being held.

'I've just received this from my brother's mother-in-law,' said Bassim, taking a letter from his pocket. 'She says that Sofia is on the verge of a breakdown. "Please help," she asks.'

Almost as soon as Bassim had left the office, a message was on its way to the Central Tracing Agency at the ICRC headquarters in Geneva, asking for their assistance. The CTA were immediately able to confirm that Faisal had been visited and registered by the ICRC. He had been discharged from hospital and was being held in one or other of the increasing number of prisoner of war camps in the area. Which one, they couldn't be certain; prisoners were continually being moved around. The CTA promised to contact the authorities in the war zone once again to see what they could do.

It was a few months later that the Red Cross tracing officer in London was able to contact Bassim and tell him where Faisal was being held. And shortly after that, Sofia wrote to Bassim that she had at last received another Red Cross Message from her husband.

As the war dragged on the Red Cross Message Service became Faisal's lifeline. He was able to write home several times, and he also sent messages to Bassim and his family in the UK. At first the messages were full of hope. 'It won't be long until we're together again' he wrote in one. And in another 'My only thought is to be able to hold you in my arms again, and hug the children.'

But with no sign of peace, the tone of Faisal's messages changed. Hope gave way to gloom. When he wrote 'For a person like me there is no difference between yesterday and today', Sofia wept openly. And when she read in another letter 'I think I am getting tired . . . This war is too long', she fell into a deep depression.

Depression gave way to desolation when, in another letter, Faisal reminded Sofia that his mother and father had both died of heart disease in their forties. Sofia collapsed after she read that Faisal was afraid that he would never see his wife and two young sons again. 'I cannot hold on much longer' he wrote. 'I thank you for your prayers.'

Sofia's mother wrote to Bassim. 'He hasn't said he has heart trouble, but I think that's because he

99

doesn't want to worry Sofia. I'm sure he's ill.'

Once again London asked Geneva for help. Sofia's mother had been right. Faisal had had a heart attack and his condition was deteriorating in prison. The ICRC doctor had asked that he be repatriated, but the request had been turned down despite the Geneva Convention dictat that seriously ill POWs should be sent home.

Faisal's captors said that if he needed medical attention there were perfectly good medical facilities in their own hospitals. Faisal became weaker. He was unable to walk for more than a few steps without stopping for breath. It was obvious that he needed immediate specialist care.

The ICRC doctors continued their requests for Faisal to be released. In their view neither the detaining country nor his own could give him the care he needed, and he should be flown to London where the surgery he required was available. Just when they sensed that their appeals were being listened to, disaster. European newspapers reported that outlawed chemical weapons were being used in the war. When the ICRC publicly protested, it was accused of unnecessary intervention: all ICRC visits to POWs, including Faisal, were banned.

The ICRC continued to press for Faisal's release. He was obviously dying, and it was apparent, even to his captors, that he would never fly again. Just in case they were successful, the British Red Cross were hard at work in London arranging his entry visa, flights, and all the other details so that if Faisal were allowed to leave, not a second would be wasted.

Months passed and everyone involved became more and more certain that Faisal was doomed to die in the hospital wing of a POW camp, somewhere in the deserts of the Middle East. Then came the fax from the ICRC with the astonishing news that Faisal had been transferred to a civilian hospital and was to be flown to Britain immediately. No one was to be informed until Faisal was safely in Britain, mainly because there had been so many failed attempts in the past.

Bassim could hardly believe his ears when almost four years after he had first approached the Red Cross for help, he heard that his brother was on a London-bound flight. He rushed to the airport with his wife and children and was there when Faisal was wheeled through Immigration. The young man's heart sank when he realized that the figure slumped in the wheelchair was the glamorous older brother he had always idolized.

'Faisal!' he cried.

'Out of the way!' a nurse shouted. 'He's just had another heart attack.'

The ambulance engine was already running as Faisal was wheeled towards it. As soon as he was safely aboard, the doors were slammed shut and the ambulance roared off into the night. It sped up the M4, siren and flashing blue light urging everything in its path to get out of the way, and it didn't stop until it reached the hospital in Cromwell Road where a team of specialists was standing by.

When Bassim and his family arrived at the hospital, it was past midnight, but the surgeons were hard at work. The night went by in a blur until a nurse came into the waiting room just as dawn was breaking over South Kensington.

'How is he?' Bassim's throat was so tight and dry that the words were almost inaudible.

'Asleep. Very weak. But we think he'll make it.'

Bassim wept like a baby.

Security was so tight that Sofia was unaware of what had been happening until a Red Crescent volunteer visited her house with the news that Faisal had been flown to England where he was now in intensive care recovering from major heart surgery.

When Sofia learned that his doctors felt that Faisal's chances of recovery would be enhanced if his wife and children were at his bedside, she stared helplessly at the Red Crescent worker, for she knew that her country did not have good relations with Britain.

'But I'll need a visa,' she sobbed. 'They won't give me a visa.'

What she didn't know was that the British Red Cross had already faxed the embassy which was looking after the UK's interests in the area:

> This is to support the application for visas for the above names whose husband/father is gravely ill, Cromwell Hospital. He was transferred from POW Camp 34X56, arrived UK Friday 26 April: had heart surgery 27. Now intensive care. Family presence urgently required.
>
> British Red Cross, London

At their end, the Red Crescent helped to obtain the necessary exit visas. A few days later, Sofia and her children were on a plane flying north-west towards

London. By the time they landed, Faisal was already out of intensive care.

Sofia held her sons' hands and they walked along the corridor towards where Bassim and his family were standing beside a closed door. 'He's in there,' said Bassim, giving her a quick embrace.

Sofia knocked on the door. Her heart was beating so loudly she almost didn't hear Faisal's whispered, 'Come in.' It was the first time in years she had heard the voice of the man she loved. She stood to the side and swung the door open so that the first thing Faisal saw was the two sons who had been little more than babies when he had been shot down.

When it was clear that Faisal was going to recover, an unasked question hung in the air; would he decide to apply to stay in Britain?

Sensing it, he volunteered, 'I'm going home, as soon as I have the all-clear. I want to touch the soil of home with my hands.'

'But they'll never let you fly again,' Bassim protested. 'Not with your heart.'

'It's not a question of flying. I have a duty. I must visit the mothers and wives of the prisoners I have left behind. I must tell them that I have seen them. Also, I know that they will find a job for me in the Air Force or the Diplomatic Service.'

Faisal went home. He had lost his health and his profession, but he still had his family and his beloved country, for which he had fought and suffered so much. He was also a great advocate for the importance of the dissemination of international humanitarian law. 'After all,' he said, 'I'm living proof that it works!'

*

Reunited!

Sadly, Faisal's suffering was not over. The fact that he had been imprisoned by the enemy country had somehow tainted him and his own government no longer trusted him. His reward for all this devotion was not to be a diplomatic post but imprisonment by his own authorities.

Streetwise but Battle Weary

It is not so long ago that Beirut was one of the most sophisticated of Mediterranean cities. Overlooking the bustling Arab centre with its ancient squares and courtyards were gleaming modern office buildings, hotels and apartment blocks. Wealthy pleasure seekers flocked to the city, to tan themselves on the sun-soaked beaches, haggle for bargains in the old souks, eat in the fashionable restaurants, and dance the night away in nightclubs as glamorous as anything Rome or Paris had to offer.

All this changed in 1975 when violent civil war broke out. For years, the world watched in stunned disbelief as shells reduced much of the city to little more than piles of rubble, and gangs of trigger-happy Muslims and Christians fought running battles in the streets. United Nations cease-fires fell apart almost as soon as they were agreed.

Most Europeans and Americans fled. The few who remained and the western journalists and television crews sent to the city to cover the war were in constant danger of being taken hostage by one or other of the warring factions.

Most of the Lebanese with money left for Paris and New York. Those who had to stay in the city scurried through the streets to buy food when they thought it was safe to go out, but mostly stayed in their houses with the sounds of thudding shells and ricochetting gunfire punctuating their waking hours.

Among those who remained was Karin Bhutan, a young divorcee, and her two children. Her separation from her husband, Kamil, had been perfectly amicable and she remained on friendly terms with him after their divorce, although she and the children saw little of him as he was actively involved in the fighting.

At first Karin was determined to sit it out, but as the war ground on and on it began to wear her down. Inflation was so high that she had difficulty in feeding herself and the two children. The last straw came in 1990 when she heard that Kamil had been taken prisoner by the Syrians whose guns had commanded key points in the country since 1978.

Kamil's presence in the war-torn city had given her some sort of security, and she had felt somehow protected by him. Now, with no idea where he was or, indeed, if she would ever see him again, she felt totally vulnerable for the first time since the fighting had begun. She decided that somehow she had to leave: she would take her children to London where she had friends on whom she knew she could depend.

Haggling for an extra pound for this, another pound for that, she sold most of what she owned, but even when she was left with little more than the clothes she stood up in she had only enough for two air fares.

One night, after she had counted the money again, praying that it had miraculously multiplied since her last tally, she sat sobbing to herself, not knowing which way to turn. She heard the doorbell, but ignored it. It rang again and again, until, wiping the tears from her eyes, Karin padded across her living-room to answer it.

'Who is it?' she called anxiously.

'Jérôme!'

Karin opened the door and fell into the arms of the old family friend she had not seen for several weeks.

'What on earth's the matter?' Jérôme's concerned voice brought tears to her eyes again.

Karin somehow pulled herself together and led Jérôme into her apartment. 'I've nothing left to sell,' she said after she had told him that Kamil's disappearance had made her decide to leave Beirut. 'I've sold everything, but I still haven't got enough for the three tickets.'

'If I could lend you – give you – the money, you know I would,' said Jérôme. 'But I've got barely enough to make ends meet as it is.'

'I know,' Karin clasped her friend's hand as she spoke. 'I know you'd help if you could.'

'Look,' said Jérôme, squeezing Karin's fingers. 'Do you mind if I make a suggestion?' Karin looked at him quizzically. 'Why don't you take little Karin with you and leave François with me? He can stay at my house for as long as it takes for you to raise enough money in England to pay for his flight.'

'I couldn't . . .'

'Don't decide now. Think about it,' said Jérôme. 'Now, have you any coffee? I'd love a cup.'

Karin didn't sleep at all that night. Several times she got up and went into the bedroom where her son and daughter lay asleep. By morning she had made up her mind . . .

'Now promise me you'll be good,' she said to François a few days later, when Jérôme came to take him to his apartment. The ten-year-old boy's thick black hair fell over his eyes as he nodded his head and said yes.

Karin relaxed on the plane, convinced that she had done the right thing. The friends she had arranged to stay with in Britain agreed with her when, a few hours later, they met her at London Airport. They were more than hospitable and promised she could live with them until she found somewhere herself.

Little Karin was astonished when for the first time in her life she was free to play out of doors for hours on end. And with no mortar fire in the background, and no danger of being shot at in the street, her mother luxuriated in the peace she had thought she would never know again. She was troubled, though, when she thought about François back in Beirut.

One of the first things she had done after she settled in was to write to him at Jérôme's address. When someone had said, 'Why don't you phone?' Karin had explained that what was taken for granted in Britain had, for years, been an undreamed of luxury in the parts of Beirut where she and Jérôme lived.

When a month passed and she hadn't heard from either Jérôme or François, she began to worry, but she wasn't too alarmed. After all, she told herself, if anything was wrong, she'd be told.

Another month, and still no word. She reassured herself that they must have written but their letters hadn't got through. And her letters had probably gone astray, too.

But as every day passed and there was still no word from Beirut, the concerns she had for her own future were outweighed by her fears for Jérôme and her son.

Eventually she could stand the silence no longer and turned to the British Red Cross for help. Could they, she begged, somehow find out if her François was all right? The British Red Cross consulted the ICRC and they in turn contacted the Red Cross in Lebanon who asked one of their volunteers to call on Jérôme's apartment when it was safe to do so.

Jérôme looked downcast at the mention of François's name. Yes, he was still living there – when he could be bothered to come home. 'He's a law unto himself, and on the streets most of the time!'

When Karin Bhutan heard the news, she was furious – with François, with Jérôme, but mostly with herself. How could she have been so foolish as to leave him behind, she asked herself over and over again. If she had tried harder, surely she could have found the money for his air fare.

Her anger turned to despair when the Red Cross told her that François had gone missing for several days after Jérôme had put his foot down and tried to assert some authority over the boy.

'Where is he now?' she asked the Red Cross volunteer who broke the news to her.

'He turned up at your Aunt Zelda's house.'

'She's not my aunt,' the despair in Karin's voice was quite clear. 'She's Kamil's mother's sister. She must be over sixty by now. And if Jérôme couldn't control my boy . . .'

She was astonished when, weeks later, she heard that François had a job working in a vegetable shop. But her hopes that the boy had turned over a new leaf were soon dashed. A few weeks later Zelda told the Red Cross that François had gone missing again.

When the Red Cross in London contacted Karin to find out if she or Kamil had any other relatives who may be sheltering François, she shook her head and begged them to try and trace her son.

Despairing of ever seeing him again, Karin lay awake night after night picturing her son's bullet-ridden body slumped in a blood-stained alley or in the bowels of a shell-shattered apartment block.

François was many things: he was lawless, he was a liar, he was a thief. But when the Red Cross eventually tracked him down, they added 'streetwise' and 'survivor' to the list.

'Where have you been living?' he was asked.

'Here and there.'

'What have you been doing?'

'This and that.'

'Don't you know you could be killed living like this?'

'Yes,' he replied. And then, his eyes shining, he added, 'That's what makes it so exciting!'

He was taken back to Zelda's house but everyone knew that it was only a matter of time before he would be back on the streets, invigorated and fascinated by the opportunities and danger that lurked there.

Perhaps a social worker could help, someone suggested to Zelda.

'Waste of time,' she scoffed. 'He should be with his mother. That's where he belongs.'

Everyone knew that this was true. But when the British Red Cross suggested this to Karin, she shrugged her shoulders helplessly.

'If he'd been with us when we arrived . . .' she sobbed when she found her voice. 'But I am not a resident here. I have been given "exceptional leave to remain", but I can't bring François here.'

'Have you asked?'

Karin shook her head. 'No! It's useless.' And then, with a glimmer of hope in her voice, she added, 'Isn't it?'

A flurry of letters and papers passed between the Red Cross and the Home Office in London and Beirut. The Lebanese Red Cross made a social report on François. He was a vulnerable minor who was not receiving proper care. He should be removed from the streets of Beirut and reunited with his mother. He had felt abandoned and his behaviour was very much a reaction to this. He had suffered the loss of both his father and his mother. On the basis of this report, the Home Office exceptionally granted permission for him to enter the UK.

In August 1992 François was flown out of Beirut bound for London to be reunited with the mother he hadn't seen for four years.

The streetwise urchin who a few months before had got his kicks out of dodging the bombs and bullets of Beirut, was soon more at home kicking a football around the playground with the other boys in the school he was enrolled in.

Today, in his spare time, he is an active and enthusiastic youth member of the Red Cross. He knows that in all likelihood had it not been for the Red Cross, his mother's worse nightmares may have come true.

Together Again – One Day Maybe

The tall, proud-featured Tigrean woman trying to keep her two children under control was plainly bewildered by the questions she was being asked by the immigration officer at London's Gatwick Airport. She had all the necessary entry documents. But the space on the landing cards, the dotted lines on which all non-European Union nationals have to write a contact address for their stay in the United Kingdom, had been left blank.

'Where have you come from?' she was asked by the intrepreter for the umpteenth time.

'Khartoum,' she replied in Tigrean. 'In the Sudan.' The woman shivered as she spoke, though whether from the chill of the frosty February morning, or because she was ill, the immigration officials couldn't say.

'And you have no idea where you are all going to live?'

'I was told we would be met.'

'The elder girl is your daughter?'

She nodded.

'And the other child?'

There was a note of weary resignation in her voice: 'Her mother is dead. She was so weak and ill, I think she has died. She could not look after little Iman.'

'And the mother's name?'
'I've told you, Chilga Gonder.'

Chilga Gonder was born in Ethiopia in 1960 in Tigre, close to the border with Eritrea. She grew up in a typical Tigrean village, helping her family to scratch a living from the land. In 1974, the emperor of Ethiopia, Haile Selasse, was deposed during a Marxist coup that plunged the country into a bitter civil war.

At first the war didn't affect Chilga. But by the time she had married and had her first baby, the area around the village had seen heavy fighting; Chilga and her husband decided that they had had enough. They trekked for days over rough, arid land before crossing into Sudan where they were granted refugee status by the United Nations High Commissioner for Refugees.

Somehow Chilga and her family survived. They were moved to a mud hut in a refugee camp south of Khartoum. Not long afterwards she gave birth to another boy and she became pregnant again when her second son was little more than a toddler. Sadly, her husband didn't live to see his third child: when Chilga was three months pregnant, he died from typhus fever. Chilga was used to death: she had seen it more times in her short life than most people will ever see it. She was heartbroken but she had her two sons to look after and, with another child on the way, life had to go on. By the time Chilga gave birth to a baby girl she called Iman, she had accepted that she was head of the family.

Conditions in the camp were primitive to say the

least: sanitation was at best basic, at worst non-existent. When Iman was still a toddler, her mother came down with fever. Somehow she found the strength to drag herself to the nearest medical centre. One look at her was enough to tell the doctors there that she had typhus.

Delirious with fever, she hovered between life and death for several weeks. Everyone agreed that even if she did recover, she would be far too weak to look after three children. The two boys were sent to live with an uncle in Qatar. He was more than happy to take in his two nephews who could help him, but was unable to offer a home to little Iman. Just when it seemed that the child would have to be put into an orphanage, Dimna Alakwazi, one of Chilga's neighbours who had been in hospital with her, offered to care for her.

Somehow Chilga pulled through. But even when she was allowed to leave the medical centre, she was still too frail to take Iman back. She lay listlessly on a blanket in her hut for hours on end, often too feeble to feed herself. Dimna now had to care for Chilga, Iman and her own children, too. No one knows who arranged for Melka to take Iman with her to Britain.

'You will be met when we get to England,' Melka said as she wrapped Iman in a cotton shawl. 'Everything will be all right. Don't worry.'

And that's how a perplexed Tigrean woman and two children came to be sitting in an immigration office at London's Gatwick Airport one cold February morning in 1990.

*

Melka and the two girls were held in a waiting room while airport staff tried to find the people who were to meet them. Their names echoed round the arrivals hall as Tannoy appeals were made for anyone waiting for Melka Tewadros to contact the nearest information desk. Nobody came forward; no one was waiting for her.

After several hours, the immigration staff contacted local social services. Melka and the two girls were taken to a bed-and-breakfast hotel near Croydon which was to be their home until more permanent accommodation could be found.

It soon became clear to social workers that Melka was not strong enough to look after two children. They managed to find a foster-mother for Iman, a Tigrean woman with children of her own, who could provide cultural continuity for the child. When she was well settled in, her social worker contacted the Red Cross. Could they find out if Iman's mother was still alive, and if she was, was there any likelihood of Iman returning to the Sudan to live with her?

The Red Cross discovered that Chilga was living alone in the same mud hut in the refugee camp. She had fully recovered, and was strong enough to hold down a part-time job as a church cleaner an hour or two's trudge from her home. Her meagre wages paid for barely half of what she needed to survive. Sudanese citizens were given ration cards that entitled them to buy staples at fixed prices. Chilga and the other refugees were having to scavenge and beg for food and clothes, or resort to the black market and pay vastly inflated prices for even the most basic foodstuffs. There was no way she could support her daughter. Nor could she ask to be resettled in Britain to be with Iman. As a settled refugee in one country, she could not be resettled in another.

Five years later Iman is still in England, living with Lila, her Tigrean foster-mother, and family. She was quick to pick up English, and is one of the brightest children in her primary school. Unfortunately, she can be a disruptive influence in the classroom. At first, her teachers put this down to cultural differences or the trauma of separation from her family, but an educational psychologist attached to the school realized that Iman is so intelligent that she feels frustrated that the rest of the class aren't as quick to learn as she is.

Through the Red Cross, Chilga and Iman have kept in touch. They have even talked to each other once or twice on the telephone. Iman was understandably guarded at first, as she had little recollection of her mother, but now, when they talk, she bubbles with news about her life in England, her school, the friends she has made and her foster family.

Perhaps the time will come when Iman can go home. Perhaps she never will. But at least, thanks to the Red Cross, mother and daughter each know where the other is, unlike thousands of Ethiopian and Eritrean refugees who, four years after the civil war ended, have no idea if their families are alive or dead.

A Chance Reunion

In October 1973, the Red Cross in London received a tracing inquiry from the Central Tracing Agency of the ICRC in Geneva asking for help in finding Leos Kodaly, a Hungarian who had fled his country during the 1956 uprising.

A routine check of the 1956 Hungarian card index – records which the British Red Cross still holds to assist with enquiries relating to those events – revealed that a Leos Kodaly had been allowed to enter Britain from an Austrian refugee camp in 1956 and in 1957 was known to be living in Yorkshire. With the search narrowed to a county, it did not take long to trace him.

'Who wants to find me?' Although he had been in England for over fifteen years, Leos still had a heavy Hungarian accent.

Meg Hobhouse, a Red Cross volunteer, slid a piece of paper across the desk and pointed to a name. 'I'm not sure how to pronounce it,' she said. 'It says that he is your cousin.'

Leos looked at the name and shook his head. 'I don't know this person.'

'Is there something wrong?' Although she had never lived in a communist bureaucracy, Meg was well aware of the fear of officialdom that lurked in the memories of those who had: it was something that lingered there for the rest of their lives.

'We don't have to tell him where you are,' she reassured Leos. 'We will only release information with your permission.'

'There's something that makes me . . .' Leos searched for a word. '. . . makes me wonder. My family is very . . .' again he stumbled '. . . unknown to me.'

It was agreed that the British Red Cross would advise the Hungarian Red Cross that Leos had been traced, but that he had requested that his whereabouts remain unknown to whoever had instituted the search as he did not know the enquirer.

'Does it work the other way around?' Leos asked Meg.

'What do you mean, "the other way round"?' said Meg. 'Is there someone there you'd like us to find?'

'Yes.' Leos spoke softly. 'I have a brother . . .'

Meg listened to Leos's story. He had been three when his mother, Erzebet, had died. Leos and his elder brother had been sent to live with foster families in different parts of the country.

'What's his name?' asked Meg.

'Stefan.'

Meg made a note of his name on her pad. 'When did you last see him?'

'Several years before the fighting started. Then, someone told me he was in some sort of trouble. He was probably sent to prison. I don't know.'

That was all Leos knew about his brother. The scant details were sent to the Tracing Service in London, where information was linked to Leos's file and Stefan's name added to the card index. But knowing that the Hungarian Red Cross was already dealing with hundreds of similar tracing requests, and because of the lack of precise information on Stefan, it was decided that it would not be possible, for the time being, to undertake enquiries.

Two years later a letter from another Hungarian refugee, Martha Bekes, arrived at the Red Cross Tracing Office in Grosvenor Crescent. Could the Red Cross trace her husband's foster-sister, Maritza, who, Martha wrote, had stayed behind in Hungary?

'My husband talks every day of seeing his sister and I know his heart aches just to see her again. So can you please tell me how I can find her for him?

'Hoping you can help. I love my husband and want to see him have the pleasure of his sister's company, if only by post.'

The case worker wrote back asking for as much information as possible about Martha's husband: where he had been born; the names of his parents; the address of the family home; any little detail that may provide a clue to where Maritza may be now.

While Red Cross tracing work requires a meticulous approach, there is at times an element of chance. By an extraordinary coincidence, when Martha Bekes's reply was put on the case worker's desk with the rest of her morning mail, she had been reading the file on Leos Kodaly. She laid it to one side and picked up Martha's letter.

Her eyes expertly scanned the answers to the many questions she had asked. Suddenly something leapt off the page: 'Stefan's mother, Erzebet, died when he was about five or six.'

119

Erzebet! Surely that was the name of Leos's mother. And hadn't she died when he was about three?

'It can't be,' she said aloud. 'That would be far too much of a coincidence. There must be thousands of women called Erzebet in Hungary.'

She picked up the file. Could Stefan Bekes be the brother Leos Kodaly was looking for? Martha had asked the Red Cross to find her husband's sister: Leos hadn't mentioned having had a sister . . . but the case worker decided to get in touch with Meg Hobhouse in Yorkshire.

A few days later, Leos was once again in Meg's office. 'We've found someone whose mother was called Erzebet and who was sent to live with foster parents at about the same time as you . . .'

'Is he my brother?' Leos was so eager that Meg prayed silently to herself this was indeed the case. 'Is it Stefan?'

'He is called Stefan. But his last name's Bekes. Not Kodaly.'

'He wasn't called Kodaly. We had different last names,' said Leos. 'Stefan and me!'

'Why didn't you tell me?' gasped Meg.

'Names don't matter. He was still my brother. Anyway, as I said, I didn't know then that you could find him.'

Meg picked up her pencil. She wrote the two names on a piece of paper, and then added 'Half-brothers?'

Martha wrote a joyful letter to say how moving it had

120

been when the two men were reunited after so many years.

'I cannot thank you enough. We thought Leos had been killed in the uprising.
'I wish you could have been there, Miss Red Cross, or should I say Miss Miracle Worker?'

Leos, too, was elated. His joy at having found Stefan again was only marred when, a month after he had asked Meg Hobhouse if the Red Cross could put him in touch with his foster parents, he was told that his father had died in 1957 and that his mother, now a confused and frail eighty-six-year-old, was confined to an old people's home. She would have no recollection of the little boy she had taken in more than fifty years before.

The Hungarian Red Cross had also been hard at work, trying to find Maritza. According to Stefan's information his sister had been courting when he had last seen her more than twenty years ago. She was probably married by now, but Stefan couldn't remember Maritza's fiancé's name.

He knew where she had been living, and where she had been working in 1956, but when the Hungarians began to look for her they found that the apartment building had been demolished and the factory had long since been closed down. No one in the area remembered Maritza.

The Hungarian Red Cross, working with sister National Societies, has helped to reunite many families separated by the traumatic events of 1956. But, sadly, no amount of searching led them to Maritza. Her present whereabouts are still unknown.

Reunited!

Maybe she died in the revolution; maybe she thinks Stefan was killed by the troops that quashed the uprising with horrifying and brutal efficiency. Perhaps she has not yet heard of the work of the Red Cross Tracing Agency. But if she ever does ask the Red Cross to help her trace her brother, all the countries that opened their doors to Hungarian refugees will be checked and a worker in Grosvenor Crescent will be able to take Stefan Bekes's file down from the shelves and stamp it CASE CLOSED – SUCCESS!

Someone to call his Own

Many refugees who resettled in the West after the Second World War desperately missed their family, friends and country. But their dread of the regimes that seized power in eastern Europe after 1945 made them afraid to make contact. They knew the mistrust with which the West was held by the authorities in many Soviet satellite states, and feared that any communication with relatives would arouse suspicion.

This was certainly what Lithuanian refugee Mikel Siakia believed. Mikel counted himself lucky to have lived through the war. For years after he was resettled in Britain, he shook with fear when he thought about his gruelling experiences, especially the night he and two of his cousins had been rounded up by German troops and bundled onto a train at gunpoint.

As it steamed southwards towards the labour camps of industrial Germany, the screams of Sofia, the little stepsister he adored, rang in Mikel's ears. She was never far from his thoughts, but when the war was over he had no way of knowing if she or any of his family had survived. And, having been separated from his cousins almost as soon as they had all been jostled off the train in Germany, he didn't know if they were alive or dead.

Reunited!

Not long after he settled in Britain, Mikel met and married Sarah Charles. He devoured what little news leaked out of Lithuania, now part of the Soviet Union, and did his best to come to terms with the fact that he would probably never see his family again. But try as he might, he couldn't hide his heartache from Sarah.

In 1974 a letter from Sarah Siakia arrived at the British Red Cross in London. How, she asked, could she go about tracing Mikel's family in Lithuania? They hadn't tried before because Mikel had been terrified that he may endanger their lives and livelihood by doing so.

The reply was reassuring. Several people had been put in touch with family in the Baltic States and, as far as the Red Cross was aware, there had been no trouble from the authorities. If Mikel would like to give them as many details as possible, they would be only too happy to do what they could.

Sarah Siakia did not write back for two months. Despite the assurances, Mikel had been reluctant to risk asking the Red Cross to contact Lithuania and had decided to take no further action, but then things had changed.

Sarah explained that for many years, she and Mikel had been caring for their mentally handicapped son, Peter William. Sadly his condition had deteriorated to the point where they had been forced to put him into a home. Mikel had taken this extremely badly. It was almost as if he blamed himself for Peter William's condition. Sarah and their other children tried their best to cheer him up, but Mikel sank into such a deep depression that Sarah felt she had to do something to rally him. It took hours of persuading, but eventually he agreed to ask the Red Cross to trace his family in Lithuania, and the two cousins he had last seen in Germany.

The Soviet Red Cross was alerted in February, and a tracing request was also sent to the International Tracing Service in Arolsen, a small village in Germany where the records kept by the former Nazi regime of the men and women who had been arrested and transported to Nazi labour camps were kept. Eight months later the Soviet Red Cross headquarters came back with word that they could find no trace of any of Mikel's relatives in Lithuania. Perhaps if they had more details . . .

However, there was better news from the International Tracing Service and in December, they were able to give Mikel the address in Germany and a photograph of Otto Neringa, one of the cousins with whom he had been deported from Lithuania.

'The news that you have located Mikel's cousin came as a great surprise and even now my husband finds it hard to believe that it can be true. I gave him the photo without your letter and he recognized him immediately even without his glasses . . .'

Sarah went on to say how grateful they both were. Mikel was almost his old self again.

Sarah wrote again two months later. Her letter made sad reading. Mikel had written time and again to the address he had been given, but had received no reply. Worse, he had been shattered by the death of

Peter William. Nothing could compensate for the boy's death, but Sarah felt that if someone could contact Mikel's cousin and ask him to write, it may cheer him up, even if only a little.

The International Tracing Service were approached again to see if they could investigate the problem. A week or two later, Mikel received another photograph of his cousin, with a letter which explained why he hadn't replied to Mikel's letters. Mikel had naturally written in Lithuanian: Otto's letter was written in German. Obviously he had forgotten his native language.

When Sarah contacted the Red Cross in London, asking them to thank their colleagues in Germany on her behalf, she told them how Mikel had sat with a German-English dictionary from four o'clock in the afternoon until almost midnight, painstakingly translating Otto's letter word by word. Mikel read that his other cousin had died in a Nazi camp, and that when the war had come to an end Otto had felt that allied-occupied Germany had more to offer him than Soviet-controlled Lithuania, so he had stayed on. He had taken rooms with Elsa and Heinrich Dettingen, a couple in Gottingen, and they had come to look upon him as one of the family.

The letter finished:

'It's been so long since I spoke Lithuanian, I've forgotten most of it. Could you write in German . . .'

Fortunately the Siakias had a German-speaking friend who was only too happy to help out. Mikel replied almost immediately and soon he and Otto were writing to each other regularly.

In 1977, the letters from Germany stopped without warning. After there had been no news for several weeks, Mikel wrote to Otto's landlady to ask if anything was wrong. When he heard that Otto had died, he was too distressed to write back himself.

Sarah replied, thanking Otto's landlady for taking the trouble of writing.

'We had been hoping that he could have come to England for our daughter's wedding and stayed on for as long as he could. Mikel would have so loved to see his cousin again . . .'

She was astonished when a few days later a parcel was delivered to her house. When she unwrapped it, she was touched to find a wedding present for her daughter from the Dettingen family. Touched, and happy, too, for the Dettingens had obviously been extremely fond of her husband's cousin.

The Red Cross found out all this when Sarah wrote to them in 1979 asking for their help in finding Erich Kupiskus, a fellow refugee of Mikel's, who had come to England with him. Erich's name was already on file at the British Red Cross Tracing Service because some relatives in Lithuania had asked the Soviet Red Cross for their help in tracing him in 1972. While enquiries are usually restricted to family members, exceptions are made for people who were in the same prison or camp. The British Red Cross was able to send Sarah Erich's address as soon as he had given his permission for them to do so.

Mikel was beginning to think that there was nothing the Red Cross couldn't do! They had found one cousin and his old friend Erich. He had never

127

quite given up hope that one day the phone would ring or a letter would land on his doormat with the news that his stepsister back in Lithuania had been traced.

Mikel suffered from periods of depression, and it was more to keep his spirits up than with any real hope of success that Sarah again contacted the Red Cross in 1982 asking if they could try once again to find Sofia. Once again the British Red Cross got in touch with the Soviet Red Cross.

After a typically thorough search, the news came back that there was no mention of Mikel's stepsister in any of their records. But, they asked, had Sarah spelt correctly the names and addresses they had been given. The names of Mikel's stepsister and the other members of his family had to be transcribed into the Cyrillic alphabet. Maybe it hadn't been Pasvalys where she'd gone to school, but Pusalots... it had all been so long ago.

Sarah wrote down all the alternatives phonetically and sent them to London. In February 1983, word came through from Moscow that the Soviet Red Cross had traced some of Mikel's cousins. They had only the vaguest memories of Mikel and had no idea where Sofia or his other stepsisters and brothers were now. They couldn't even be sure that they had lived to see the end of the war.

Mikel's mood swung like a pendulum; Sarah had to cajole him into writing to his cousins, via the Red Cross, asking for a clue, anything at all that could lead him to his stepbrothers and sisters, especially Sofia. He was still desperately afraid that he would land his cousins in trouble, but he wrote a very guarded letter to Lithuania via the Red Cross in London.

No sooner had the letter been forwarded to Lithuania, than Sarah wrote again with the most extraordinary news. A Lithuanian friend of Mikel's had casually picked up a newsletter aimed at emigrés from the Baltic States who were living in London. As he was flicking through it, his eye was caught by a grainy photograph, obviously taken many years before, of a shy young man squinting at the camera. Below it was an appeal from an elderly woman living in Vilnius, who was looking for her stepbrother Mikel who had never come back from the war.

The more he looked at the photograph the more familiar it seemed. Something about the way the mouth turned up, the expression in the eyes. Surely, he said to himself, that's Mikel . . .

As soon as he could he was on the phone, and the next morning the editor of the newsletter wrote to the woman in Vilnius to tell her that her brother may have been found.

A few weeks later, a letter from Sofia arrived on the Siakias' doormat. Mikel broke down when he read that all his stepbrothers and sisters were still alive and living in Lithuania. The very next day a letter from the Soviet Red Cross was received in London with the news that the additional information Mikel had given them had enabled Red Cross workers to trace his family.

Christmas 1984 was one of the most memorable that Sarah and Mikel Siakia had ever spent. After months of agonized waiting, Sofia had been given an exit visa and was able to come to London to see her brother for the first time in over forty years. She was joined a week or two later by another brother, Constantin. In a letter to the British Red Cross, Sarah wrote:

'The start of 1985 was the happiest of happy new years for us all, especially Mikel. You gave him something he had yearned for since I have known him: someone of his own. Thank you.'

The Experts' Opinion

Maria Taylor has never forgotten the day the letter arrived. It was addressed to her father and dated 2 May 1943. As he read it, the straight-backed Austrian seemed to crumble into himself and age visibly before his daughter's eyes. He slumped into a chair, the tears streaming down his face.

'Papa!' the teenage girl cried, running to his side. 'What's the matter, Papa?'

The old man said nothing. The letter fell from his hand and landed at Maria's feet. She stopped to pick it up, her father's tears had smudged the peacock blue ink, but the words were still quite legible:

'. . . I regret to have to inform you that your son Hans von Braun is missing, believed to have been killed in action . . .'

Hans was twenty-two. In 1938, after the Anschluss when Austria became a province of the Third Reich, he had been conscripted into the German army. Five years later, in February 1943, his unit was involved in a long, drawn-out battle in eastern Poland. Hans, Maria read, had been riding pillion on a motorbike, part of a convoy trying to make it back behind German lines. As she read what happened next she pictured the scene in her mind's eye when the convoy was ambushed by a Russian cavalry unit, and she could almost hear the machine-gun fire rip through the air, drowning out the roar of the German trucks and bikes as they tried to accelerate to safety.

Hans's companion had been seriously injured and taken prisoner when their bike slewed off the frozen track and slammed into a tree.

Maria's shaking hand turned the letter over and she read that there was no news of Hans. Three months had passed since the skirmish, and his name had not appeared on any lists of German soldiers taken prisoner by the Russians. The territory was still in Russian hands so it had been impossible for the Germans to search the area for bodies or any survivors who had somehow managed to evade capture and who may still have been in hiding behind Russian lines.

The letter finished with an assurance that should any further news become available, Hans's family would be duly informed.

Maria tried to comfort her father but he was inconsolable. 'He's dead,' he mumbled over and over again. 'Hans is dead.'

'Maybe not,' whispered Maria. 'We don't know for sure. Maybe he's still alive somewhere. Maybe he's been taken prisoner.'

But the old man ignored her. 'He's dead,' he wept. 'Hans is dead.'

When the war came to an end there was still no news of Hans, until one day Frederic Schultz, an old friend of his and a fellow conscript newly released by the Allies, called on the von Brauns.

'Did Hans make it home?' he asked.

Maria shook her head. 'No,' she said softly. 'He went missing in 1943. Believed dead.'

'Where?'

'Somewhere in eastern Poland,' said Maria and told the young man about the letter they had received. 'I still have it.'

'But I was in the same convoy. Hans was thrown clear of the bike when it crashed and I saw him run into the undergrowth.'

'You mean he got away?' Maria gasped.

Frederic frowned. 'I think so,' he said. 'Certainly, his body wasn't among those we found when we forced the Russians back and retook the area.'

From that day on, Maria refused to believe that her brother was dead. At first, she thought he was probably being held by the Allies and there had been some sort of delay in his being released. Then, when she heard rumours that the Russians were holding thousands of German soldiers in labour camps, she thought that he must be somewhere in Soviet-held territory.

For most Austrians, the dark days of post-war austerity seemed to last for ever. But a year or two after the war, Maria fell in love with a British national serviceman who was with the occupying forces. Maria married her soldier and when he was sent back to Britain, she went with him.

She was understandably nervous when she arrived in England. She had no idea how she would be received. After all, she thought to herself, it wasn't so long ago that England and Austria had been at war.

She needn't have worried. As far as her husband's family and friends were concerned, if Maria was good enough for their Tom, she was good enough for them. And if any of her new neighbours resented living alongside an Austrian, they hid their animosity completely, for neither Maria nor Tom heard as much as a whisper of ill-feeling.

Maria was soon so busy setting up home and, later, bringing up her children that she had little time to dwell on the past. But she often thought of the brother who had never come home from the war, and as neither she nor her parents had ever had official confirmation that he was dead, deep in her heart, she felt he was still alive.

Tom discouraged her from clinging to this belief, but as time passed finding Hans became more and more important to Maria.

It was not until February 1982 that she plucked up the courage to ask the Red Cross if there was any chance that they could trace the brother she had not seen for over forty years.

'Do you know his army number?' she was asked by Helen Cosway, the Red Cross volunteer who was assigned to her case.

'No,' she replied, but told Helen what she knew of the regiment her brother had been fighting with when he had gone missing.

The British Red Cross sent these sketchy details to the Red Cross in what was then West Germany. It took only a month for the German Red Cross to come back with the news that there was no Hans von Braun listed in any of the records they held of those killed or listed as missing during the war.

Maria's reaction when the Red Cross told her this was one of complete astonishment. 'But I still have the letter from his commanding officer,' she said. 'I showed it to you last time we talked.'

'I know,' Helen's voice was calm and soothing. 'That's why the German Red Cross have passed the information on to the Army Records Office in Berlin and to the Red Cross in Moscow.'

'How long will it take for them to check their records?' asked Maria.

'There's a huge backlog in Moscow,' said Helen. 'I shouldn't expect we'll hear from them for at least twelve months, maybe longer. I'm sorry it will take so long. The German Red Cross should come back to us before that, though.'

'My dear,' Maria smiled. 'I have waited for forty years, another few months isn't going to make much difference.'

The German Red Cross confirmed with the ICRC in Geneva that there was no mention of Hans von Braun in any of their Second World War POW records. But they were puzzled by the case. Hans's commanding officer had written that the young Austrian had gone missing in battle, so surely his name must be in some archive somewhere.

Some of the German Red Cross workers are military historians who specialize in researching Second World War battles in Poland. They checked records of soldiers who, like Hans, had been reported missing in the area in 1943 but who had turned up after the war. They also studied war diaries, journals and maps of the area where Hans had last been seen. With the help of statements taken from ex-soldiers who had fought in the area, they reconstructed the Russian attack on Hans's convoy and came to the conclusion that Hans had died, either in the ambush on 2 February 1943 or a few days afterwards, and somehow in the confusion that had followed, he had never been officially posted as dead or missing.

By the time the German Red Cross experts' opinion arrived at the British Red Cross headquarters in London, the Soviet Red Cross had also confirmed that there was no Hans von Braun in any of their records.

The report from the German Red Cross was the first confirmation that Hans was dead, and this news had to be conveyed personally.

Helen went to Maria's house with the report from Berlin. 'May I read it?' Maria asked when the news was broken to her.

Helen handed the papers to the older woman whose hands trembled as she read what the German Red Cross had written.

The report contained a detailed description of the military action and a vivid and harrowing account of the battle and of the freezing conditions in which it had been fought. It went on:

'Enquiries have shown that many of those who were reported missing were killed in the skirmish. Others, however, probably froze to death in the thick snow, or slipped into the [river] Donez and drowned. All our investigations lead us to the conclusion that Hans von Braun was either killed in action or died in the aftermath.'

'You are the next of kin. This statement requires your signature as agreement to the contents. On this basis a death certificate will be issued for Hans,' Helen explained to Maria.

A few days later, Helen reported back to the

British Red Cross in London. The lengths the German Red Cross had gone to and the way they had reported the results of their investigation had helped convince Maria that Hans was really dead. What she found difficult to come to terms with, Helen wrote, was that there was no grave she could stand at and say a silent farewell to her brother.

When Maria wrote to the Red Cross to thank them for all the work they had done, she finished her letter:

'Perhaps it would have been better if Frederic had not told us he had seen Hans escape. To have lived for so long with the hope that he may still be alive and now to have to bid him farewell in my heart after all these years is something I find hard to do. But thank you all for helping me through this – especially Helen. She has been a strong support to me, and has understood my feelings. And I know I can ring her any time I need to talk about it.'

Don't Tell Them Where I Am

The most frustrating thing from the tracing volunteer's point of view is not when after a long, arduous search hopes soar that they are on the verge of success and are then dashed at the last minute: it's when they find someone only to be told, 'I don't want you to tell them where I am.'

There's little the Red Cross volunteer can do. They have to respect the person's wish to be left alone . . . but they can talk about how much information can be conveyed.

In 1956, Istvan and Agnes fled Hungary and were offered a new start in life in Britain. Like thousands of other Hungarian refugees they left their children, Lila and Franz, behind them, intending to send for them once they had settled down.

Istvan and Agnes found it very hard to adapt to their new life and it wasn't long before the stress started to show on their marriage. Little squabbles led to rows which often resulted in angry, fretful silences that lasted for days on end. It was no one's fault: the strain of leaving their home, saying goodbye to family and friends, the bewildering differences between Britain and Hungary, the uncertainty of what the future held for them and, most important of all, the pain of being parted from the children had frayed their nerves to breaking point.

When Agnes told her husband that she had fallen in love with another man, the row raged for hours and only ended when she threw some clothes into her shopping bag and stormed out of the house saying she was going to stay with friends. When Istvan calmed down, he realized that his anger had been caused by hurt pride more than anything else.

When Agnes came home a few days later to collect the rest of her things she was extremely wary of Istvan. But Istvan was cool towards her, almost to the point of indifference. Even when she told him that she was planning to emigrate to Canada as soon as she had married her boyfriend, he agreed without protest to a divorce.

'And Lila and Franz?' he asked. 'In Hungary.' And for the first time there was anger in his voice. Anger and apprehension.

'You know that Kadar lets no one leave now.'

'And if he ever does?' Istvan's voice was raised.

Britain in the 1950s was a very different place from Britain in the 1990s when divorce is more or less automatic for a couple who have lived apart for two years. Then it was a long, involved, cumbersome process often involving subterfuge and collusion. Agnes knew that Istvan, if he set his mind to it, could destroy her future happiness. Without a divorce she couldn't marry Egon and without a marriage certificate Egon and she couldn't emigrate to Canada together.

'If he ever does, then maybe Mama and Papa could bring them to Canada . . .'

'No!' Istvan had regained his composure. His voice was cold and uncompassionate. 'If they are ever allowed to leave, they come here. If you don't agree . . .'

When Istvan broke the seemingly endless silence and said again, 'If you don't agree . . .' Agnes, knowing full well what he was threatening, bit her lip and sighed, 'Very well!'

As soon as Agnes had the decree absolute, she married Egon and sailed to Canada.

A month or two later, Istvan heard from Hungary that his mother had been rushed to hospital with a suspected embolism and was not expected to recover. Lila and Franz had been taken into a children's home.

Istvan, desperately worried that if his mother died his children would be put up for adoption, turned to the British Council for Aid to Refugees for help. The Refugee Council asked the Red Cross if they could do anything to put Istvan's mind at rest. The Red Cross in London contacted the Hungarian Red Cross asking them for a welfare report on the grandmother and the children.

The Hungarian Red Cross reported that Istvan's mother had surprised everyone and pulled through. Lila was back living with her, but Franz had been sent to live with foster parents because doctors thought that two children would be too much for his grandmother.

When the Red Cross told him the good news about his mother, Istvan was obviously relieved, but plainly there was still something worrying him. When pressed, he told the Red Cross that he was scared that Agnes's parents would use his mother's ill-health as an excuse to try somehow to arrange for the children to leave Hungary and join their mother in Canada.

Sure enough, the following year, by which time Istvan had moved house, the Canadian Red Cross sent an enquiry to the British Red Cross asking for help in tracing Istvan.

The Canadian Red Cross, it emerged, had been baffled to receive a letter from Agnes's father in Hungary claiming that he had been told by the Red Cross that Lila was to be allowed to leave Hungary. The Canadians were well aware that the Hungarian border with the West had long been closed, and that no family reunions were taking place as no one was allowed to leave. Had the Hungarians had a change of heart and been persuaded on humanitarian grounds to make an exception in Lila's case?

The Canadian Red Cross also sent an envelope addressed to Istvan containing a letter from Agnes's father in Hungary. The old man had no idea where his former son-in-law was now living so he had written to him care of Agnes in Canada, in case she had a current address for her ex-husband.

It wasn't too difficult for the Red Cross to trace Istvan at his new address because at that time under British law all aliens were required to report regularly to their nearest immigration office. A few days after the request was received in London, Red Cross volunteer Mamie Gillespie was able to hand over the letter to Istvan in person.

Istvan was obviously furious with what he read. 'Agnes agreed that if Lila was ever allowed to leave, she would come here,' he said through clenched teeth. 'Now, she uses her father to try to get me to change my mind.'

'And will you?' One look at the expression on Istvan's face answered Mamie's question.

Mamie Gillespie wrote back to Canada that as far as the British Red Cross was aware, the only passports and exit visas being issued in Hungary were to diplomats and embassy officials being sent on tours of duty on other countries or to businessmen on officially sponsored export missions overseas. She also wrote that Istvan considered himself to be his daughter's legal guardian, and would never allow Lila to live with Agnes in Canada should the possibility ever arise.

Later that year, the Canadian Red Cross wrote back to London with a request that they get in touch with Istvan again and give him another letter as he seemed to have moved. Again, Mamie was there when he opened it.

'Is it anything we can help with?' she asked.

'She's asking me to sign this,' said Istvan handing Mamie the piece of paper that had been neatly folded inside the letter. Mamie saw at once what it was: a legally binding document carefully worded as if it had been written by Istvan waiving any claims to custody over Lila should the little girl ever be allowed to leave Hungary.

Mamie reported back to the Tracing Department that not only had Istvan refused to sign the paper, but he had been so incensed by what Agnes had done, he had decided to do everything he could to get Lila out of Hungary. He had, in fact, asked Mamie to help him. The British Red Cross learned a few months later that, against all the odds and completely out of the blue, Lila had been given an exit visa.

142

The Canadian Red Cross was almost immediately back in touch with the British Red Cross. Agnes had heard from her father that Lila had been allowed to leave the country. Now she had no idea where Istvan had taken her. Could the Red Cross track them down, and find out how Lila was?

The British Red Cross knew very well where they were, but Istvan steadfastly refused to give permission for his address to be revealed, and there was nothing anyone could say to make him change his mind. When the Canadian Red Cross told Agnes this, she was distraught. Soon her distress gave way to anger, and anger to a staunch determination that one day she would have Lila by her side.

Meanwhile, Istvan did his best to give Lila a good home, but it soon became clear that the task of bringing up the little girl was too much for him. Lila was taken into care and then fostered. When Istvan was asked by the Red Cross for permission to let Agnes know what had happened, he reluctantly agreed.

Life seemed to get on top of him after that. In 1961, Agnes sent Lila a six-week excursion air ticket to Canada. Although she was still with her foster parents and legally under council care, Istvan was approached by social workers and asked if he had any objections to Lila spending the summer in Canada. He didn't even bother to go to the airport to see his excited seven-year-old daughter off.

He was equally unconcerned when the same social workers broke the news to him two months later that Lila was still in Canada and Agnes had been granted permission to keep her there. The file concerning Istvan and Lila was closed.

The Past is a Foreign Country

In the days before travel between eastern and western Europe became as easy, in some cases easier, than getting from Edgware to Morden on London's Northern Line, it could take years for the Red Cross to organize exit visas, passports and the other documents needed to get someone out of Soviet-controlled countries to be reunited with family in the West.

It was just as difficult and time-consuming for the Red Cross to arrange the entry visas and the mountain of other papers required by refugees who wanted to go home . . .

Maria Antonescu was a toddler when the First World War came to an end in Romania. The interwar years there were marked by deep anti-communist suspicion and a succession of right-wing coups, but life carried on as it had for centuries in the villages of the Moldavian Highlands where Maria and her family lived. So it wasn't until 1941 when Romania joined in the German invasion of Russia that the outside world impinged on Maria and her family.

The struggle for survival became even worse after 1944 when the Russians counter-attacked. As Stalin's troops advanced, Maria and thousands of other Romanians said goodbye to their families and trekked west to get as far away from the Russian guns as possible. When peace came Maria found herself in allied-controlled Germany and needed little persuasion to accept a passage to Britain and a new start in life.

Shortly after she arrived at Harwich, she was sent to a resettlement camp near Bradford, where she met and married a hard-working, down-to-earth York-shireman. Her letters home were full of news about how different life was in England. Her husband had a steady job in the wool mills and there was more than enough money to pay the rent on their little terrace-house. Most food was rationed, but potatoes, flour and some other staples were off the coupons so there was usually enough to go round, especially after her husband took over an allotment where he grew enough vegetables to feed a family of six, never mind a couple on their own. And, to Maria's great delight, there was a cinema just along the road that showed three different films every week.

For a woman who had spent most of her life in rural Romania and then endured years of wartime privation, things could hardly be better. When her letters reached home, usually months after Maria had written them, her family were delighted that she was so happy, for if life had been tough in Romania during the war, it was almost as bad after the Communists took over in 1948.

After a few years Maria's letters suddenly stopped. Her three brothers and four sisters wondered what had happened, but they had other worries and it wasn't until 1968 that Johanna Antonescu wrote to the Red Cross in Bucharest with the address that had been on Maria's last letter, asking if anything could be done to find out what had happened to her sister.

When the British Red Cross received the tracing request from the Romanian Red Cross, they asked their Branch in Yorkshire to make enquiries at the last known address.

The rows of little terrace-houses where Maria had lived had been demolished in the Macmillan government housing boom and replaced by a typical 1950s housing estate of trim little semi-detached houses, each with a strip of garden back and front.

After weeks of fruitless and frustrating leads, Peggy Scott, one of the volunteers who spent most of her free time on the search for Maria Antonescu, tracked down a woman who had known Maria.

'I don't suppose you have any idea where they are now?' Peggy Scott asked.

'They? Maria was on her own when I knew her,' said the woman.

'You mean before she was married?'

'No. She was divorced. Knocked her sideways it had, I shouldn't think she ever got over it. Never stopped crying. Stopped looking after herself. That's why they took her away in the end.'

'Took her away?' echoed Peggy. 'Do you know where?'

'Sorry,' said the woman. 'I've got no idea where she went.'

Further enquiries failed to reveal where Maria was, so the British Red Cross had to report their lack of success to date to the Romanian Red Cross. But maybe, they wrote, if the family could supply further details about either Maria or her family, they could continue with the search.

146

No more was heard until 1972, when Joanna Antonescu wrote again saying the family consisted of three brothers and four sisters and they all wanted news of their sister in England. The British Red Cross was asked to make further enquiries.

With this extra information, Peggy Scott was able to continue her search. She succeeded in finding out that Maria was a long-term patient in an asylum, although she was now more institutionalised than mentally disturbed.

'Actually,' the matron told Peggy. 'If she had any family, she could have gone to live with them years ago.'

'She's got nobody in this country?'

'Not really. In fact we don't know much about her,' said the matron. 'She refused to talk to anyone for months after she first came here. She still doesn't talk much. We've just picked up bits and pieces about her from the little she says.'

'Would she remember her family in Romania?'

'We could ask her,' the matron said. 'But I'll have to put it to Doctor Wilkinson first. See what he says.'

A few days later, the matron called Peggy and told her that when Maria had been asked if she had a sister called Johanna, she had nodded slowly, and, rocking her chair backwards and forwards, had softly repeated the name over and over again.

When Johanna heard from the Romanian Red Cross that Maria was a patient in a mental hospital she was very distressed. 'She should be here,' she cried. 'With her family. At home.' Then she stopped weeping and said, 'Could we do that? Bring Maria home?' They promised to seek the advice of the British Red Cross.

Reunited!

When the Red Cross put Johanna's idea to Maria's doctors, they said it was an excellent idea. 'She'd need looking after, of course,' Doctor Wilkinson said. 'But if the family wish to have her with them, there's no reason why we shouldn't start looking at the possibilities of her going.'

The Red Cross in London and Bucharest promised to do whatever they could to get Maria home, but the problems seemed insurmountable. She needed a passport, an entry visa into Romania and permission from the Romanian authorities to settle there. The questions the Romanian officials asked seemed endless; the procedures never ending.

It was not until the winter of 1973 that Maria had her passport and an entry visa that allowed her to stay in Romania for as long as she wanted.

Johanna and the rest of the family pooled what little money they had but still didn't have enough to pay to get Maria to Romania. Johanna wrote to a relative who had settled in Canada after the war asking for help. He had fond memories of his cousin and said he would be only too happy to pay the fare. It took some time for him to arrange to get the money out of Canada, and it was in February 1974 that Maria, with her few possessions packed into a small suitcase, boarded a plane bound for Bucharest.

Johanna was at the airport to meet her sister. She hadn't quite known what to expect. Or what she would feel. The grey-haired woman's face was quite expressionless and she had merely nodded when Johanna stepped forward and said, 'Maria?'

She tried to talk to her sister on the journey home but Maria, obviously exhausted from her long flight, said little and soon dropped off.

For weeks she seemed suspicious of the outside world. She said little, ate what was put in front of her without comment, and was reluctant to leave the simply-furnished room Johanna had prepared for her, even to visit her family who all lived close by.

Maria didn't need a lot of looking after, but even so Johanna began to wonder if bringing her sister home had been such a good idea. Maria hadn't spoken Romanian for many years and found it difficult to understand what was being said to her. She was confused – but gradually the barrier between Maria and the rest of the world began to disappear: she started to to settle into her new life and began to take an interest in what was happening around her.

After a few months she was quite at home. The two sisters spent many a happy evening chatting about their childhood and chewing over titbits of family news. Maria began to enjoy the company of her nephews and nieces and their children, but whenever anyone mentioned England, Yorkshire, the broken marriage or her long years in the home, Maria lapsed into silence and her eyes seemed glaze over. When the British Red Cross requested a report on how things were going, Johanna said that it was as if Maria had taken a rubber and erased from her mind everything to do with her previous life in England that had been etched there.

And when Johanna was asked if all the work it had taken to arrange for Maria to return to Romania, and the months of stress of settling her in had been worth while she said, 'Of course it was. People belong with their families, don't they? In the long run, family is all that matters.'

The Detainee's Parcel

In 1912, when war flared in the Balkans, the Red Cross in Belgrade was given permission to send 'material comforts' and money to prisoners of war. Since then, the provision of Red Cross parcels has become a traditional and well-known part of its work. What is not so well known is that parcels have been sent not just to prisoners of war but to civilian detainees, too. Among such recipients were civilians of various nationalities detained in Maoist China. Parcels were sent to them throughout the 1950s, 60s and in one special case for more than twenty-five years, up to 1978.

When the Korean War came to an end in 1953, the Chinese authorities agreed to accept Red Cross parcels for the American POWs they still held, but only on condition that a member of the Hong Kong Branch of the British Red Cross was at the border when the parcels were handed over to the Chinese Red Cross. There were precise and strictly monitored stipulations as to how heavy and how large the parcels could be and what they could contain. Each one was thoroughly searched and the Red Cross was well aware that any deviation from the rules would give the Chinese an excuse to refuse to accept any more parcels.

It was dangerous work. The Chinese Red Cross workers who accepted the parcels were escorted to the border by armed guards. With guns trained on them, the volunteers on both sides were painfully aware that one wrong step could provoke a volley of gunfire from the obviously nervous and suspicious Chinese troops.

Eventually, the Chinese government agreed that civilian detainees as well as captive servicemen could receive Red Cross parcels. In each case, permission had to be obtained through the Chinese Red Cross, and the British Red Cross worked closely with the Hong Kong Branch. The whole operation was anxiously monitored by Muriel Monkhouse in London. Even after all the American prisoners of war had been repatriated, she kept an eagle eye on the situation in China. As the years passed the civilian detainees were either released or died until their number had dwindled.

One man known to the British Red Cross was Sergei Czerney, a Russian who had been born in Shanghai in 1906. When he was still a toddler, his mother travelled abroad for a while, eventually reaching San Francisco. Subsequently, the political situation in China made it dangerous for her to return, so she settled in the United States, hoping that Sergei, his sister Aylsa and their father could eventually join her there. But Sergei's father decided that he and his son would stay put, and it was only Aylsa who sailed from Shanghai to California.

Sergei wrote to his mother and sister regularly, and even during the civil war that engulfed China in the 1940s, he managed to get letters out of the

151

country to the States. But in 1952 the letters suddenly stopped.

At first Madame Czerney wasn't too anxious: she knew how things were in China. But as the months passed and there was still no news, she became more and more worried and eventually so distracted that Aylsa became concerned for her mother's mental health.

When the next letter eventually came, Madame Czerney didn't know whether to laugh because at last her son had written, or to cry because she read that he had fallen foul of the law and was under house arrest. It was a miracle that he had managed to get a letter out of the country.

Madame Czerney knew that if anyone could help it was the Red Cross. She wrote the first of a stream of impassioned letters to the Hong Kong Branch of the British Red Cross begging them to help get her son out of China. Meanwhile, Aylsa, who had become an American citizen, bombarded the US State Department with requests that they do something to help.

In Grosvenor Crescent in London, Muriel Monkhouse was still very much involved with the way things were in China, but there was not a great deal she could do apart from satisfy herself that Sergei was still allowed to receive Red Cross parcels. When word came through from Hong Kong that Sergei's health was rapidly deteriorating, Muriel contacted the American Red Cross and asked them to do whatever they could to encourage Sergei's family to keep up their campaign to have him released.

Over the years, the American Red Cross and Aylsa came to know Muriel very well through her letters.

152

Wryly humorous and needle-sharp in their obser-
vations, they impressed everyone who read them,
including officials at the State Department who
made every diplomatic effort they dared to intervene
on Sergei's behalf. But the Chinese government
refused to release him.

Sergei's only contact with the outside world was
via the Red Cross and their parcels. At times, the
Chinese appeared to be on the point of refusing to
accept them but, despite the danger, Red Cross
volunteers from Hong Kong continued to keep their
rendezvous with their Chinese counterparts to make
sure that Sergei got his parcels.

For Sergei, the parcels were more than a regular
supply of much-needed tinned food, they were a
beacon blazing with the message that he had not
been forgotten by the outside world.

The 1960s swung into the 1970s and there was still
no sign of Sergei being released. As the years passed,
Alysa and her mother became more and more
desperate. At the same time Muriel, who was due to
retire at the end of 1978, became more determined
that if it was the last thing she did before she
relinquished her duties, she would get Sergei out of
China.

Early in 1978, Aylsa decided to fly to London to
meet Muriel who, she felt, was her strongest ally. She
wanted to see if together they could make one last
attempt to free Sergei. They talked for a long time
and Alysa remembers crying throughout their
meeting. Muriel promised that she would continue to
work in tandem with the American Red Cross to
maintain contact.

When she was back in the United States, Aylsa

badgered the Red Cross and the State Department and eventually enlisted the support of several powerful voices in the Senate. Just before Christmas in 1978, completely out of the blue, the Chinese relented and Sergei was released. Muriel still treasures the letter she received from Alysa, and always will.

Sergei was flown to Hong Kong where he was met by Red Cross volunteers. He was emaciated and disoriented and it was three months before he was strong enough to travel to the States where Madame Czerney, who was now ninety, and Alysa were waiting with the Red Cross to greet him when he was helped off the plane. The old lady broke down when she embraced the son she had last seen being held aloft by his nurse waving goodbye. The baby had become an old man, well into his seventies and, judging from his grey skin and rasping breath, he was far from well.

Aylsa was well aware that had it not been for Muriel, she and her mother would probably have given up and Sergei would never have been released. She begged Muriel to promise that if she was ever in the States, she would visit them all in San Francisco.

Muriel had already planned a trip to America in 1979 to visit friends and Red Cross colleagues. She was delighted to add San Francisco to her itinerary and when she arrived, she was as overwhelmed by the warmth of the family's welcome as they were overjoyed to see her.

Sergei had been fitted with a pacemaker and was in fine fettle. Muriel was astonished at how calm he was, how gentle and how amazingly unbitter that twenty-five years of his life had been stolen from him. It was obvious that a deep spirituality had enabled him to withstand a quarter of a century of virtual isolation. She was also amazed at how the same tranquillity had allowed him to take the hustle and bustle of twentieth-century America with its shopping malls, traffic jams and noisy teenagers in his stride.

A few months later, when Muriel was back in London, she received a postcard from Mexico. It was the first of many from the brother and sister. Aylsa, always an enthusiastic traveller, was determined to show her brother as much of the world as possible. They were constantly flying here and there, until 1986 when Muriel heard from Aylsa that Sergei had died of a massive heart attack. He had always been, Alysa wrote, absolutely certain that had it not been for the Red Cross he would never have been released.

No praise can be too high for the Hong Kong Red Cross members who, over those long years, never failed to deliver the parcels on time each month. Their reward, however, must surely be Sergei's often repeated words, 'The Red Cross parcels saved my life.'

An Exception to the Rules

When Diana Barry got in touch with the Manchester Branch of the Red Cross and asked for their help in putting her neighbour in touch with the family she hadn't seen since she left Poland almost fifty years before, she was told that it was extremely rare for the Red Cross to undertake tracing requests on behalf of third parties who were not related in any way. But Diana was quite persistent.

'You see,' she told Betty Walker, 'Antonia doesn't know I'm asking . . .'

'Why not?'

'Because if she knew we were looking and didn't find them, I'm not sure she could stand it.'

'In that case,' said Betty. 'Wouldn't it be kinder to leave well alone? After all, if your friend's family were still alive, maybe they would have tried to contact her.'

'Maybe. But they probably think she died in the war and didn't think it worth while.'

Betty said nothing.

'Oh please,' Diana begged. 'She's been such a good friend to me. It would mean so much to her if we – you, I suppose – could find them. Please!'

Betty was well aware that the fall of Communism had encouraged a flood of tracing enquiries from East and West, and that Red Cross volunteers were already struggling to cope. She knew she should be firm with Diana . . . but she picked up her pen and began to note what Diana knew about Antonia and her family in Poland . . .

Antonia Sobieski was seventeen when the Nazis marched into the town in the east of the country where she lived with her parents and three sisters. It was Anya, the eldest child who had been earmarked by the Germans for deportation to a labour camp in the Ruhr valley, but when they came for her she was so heavily pregnant that it was Antonia who had been dragged screaming from the flat to the lorry below.

Somehow she survived the hardships of the labour camp. She endured years of bestial cruelty at the hands of the overseers who took sadistic pleasure in their work. She managed to scurry to the safety of the air raid shelters just in time during the allied bombing raids which became increasingly frequent as the war went on.

After the fall of Berlin and the end of the war in Europe, Antonia was asked if she wanted to return to her home in Poland or if she would like the chance to be resettled in Britain.

She knew that her Poland was now part of the Soviet Union, so she decided to make a new start, and was given travel documents and a ticket for England.

After years of being bullied and beaten, Antonia found it difficult to adapt to the kindness of strangers. More than once when someone held out a welcoming hand to her, she instinctively shied away from it, expecting to feel its full force across her face at any minute. She was so conditioned by her deep fear of being singled out by the Nazis, that even years later whenever she heard her name being called out, she had to screw up every ounce of courage before she answered.

Among those in the resettlement camp who understood exactly how she felt was Mieszko Pilsuski, a fellow Pole from Gdansk. Antonia found his sympathetic words and gentle, encouraging smiles oh so comforting, and was soon spending most of her free time in his company.

When Mieszko was offered a job in Manchester, he asked Antonia to go with him.

'Do you mean to keep house for you?' she asked.

'Yes!' he smiled, teasingly.

'To wash and cook for you?'

He laughed and said, 'Isn't that what wives do for their husbands in Britain?'

'You mean you want to marry me? Why didn't you come right out and ask me?'

A few days after their wedding, Antonia and Mieszko travelled to the north of England to begin their new life together. They had been told that northerners were friendly people, but that hadn't prepared them for the warmth of the welcome they received, especially from Diana Barry, who lived next door but one to the terrace-house that came with Mieszko's job.

They had no sooner moved in, than Diana was there to see if there was anything they needed. And she was back again the following Monday after Mieszko had gone to work when she knew Antonia would be on her own for the first time and may be feeling lonely. 'Now, you put the kettle on,' she said to Antonia. 'And once we've had a cup of tea, I'll show you where the shops are, and where to get your coupons and things. And if there's anything you need, remember I'm just two doors down the road.'

Antonia doesn't know how she would have coped without Diana. If she was feeling down, Diana always managed to cheer her up. If she had something on her mind, Diana was there with an understanding ear and down-to-earth advice. It was Diana who had pulled a twopenny bit from her apron pocket and run to the phone box to summon the midwife when Antonia's labour pains started weeks before they were due. It was Diana who looked after the children when Antonia had to go into hospital to have her appendix removed. And it was to Diana that Antonia turned for comfort when her eldest son, Stanislas, died of chickenpox when he was just eighteen.

It wasn't a one-sided relationship, for Antonia was always there whenever Diana needed someone to talk to or a shoulder to cry on.

Antonia very rarely talked about the past either to Diana or, when they had grown up, to her children. They knew that she would have loved to know what had happened to her family, but whenever anyone suggested trying to find them, Antonia would say, 'It's too long ago. Far too long ago.'

In 1990 Diana read how the fall of Communism had made it easier for the Red Cross to reunite families that had been scattered by the war. After discussing it with Antonia's children, she decided to take matters into her own hands and went into the Red Cross office in Manchester.

Betty Walker's notes were passed to London and, via the ICRC in Geneva, on to Poland where they were added to the vast number of tracing cases the Red Cross was already working on. Polish volunteers did what they could locally, but there was no mention of Anya or Antonia's two younger sisters in the records of those listed as missing or killed during the war. Experienced volunteers working on the case knew that even though many new records had come to light, the lists were far from complete. Despite this, they were reasonably certain that had all three sisters died, they would have found the name of at least one of them in some file or other.

The Polish Red Cross suspected that if the three sisters were still alive, they could well be living in one of the fifteen new states that had been created out of the former USSR, most likely Byelorussia.

Given that fifty-three years had elapsed since Antonia had last seen her family, the Byelorussian Red Cross decided that time was of the essence, and they decided to publicise the story in the newspapers. Anyone whose sister Antonia Sobieski had been sent to a German labour camp in 1941 was asked to contact them or write to her c/o Diana Barry in Manchester.

Diana didn't have an inkling that her name had appeared in the Byelorussian newspapers. She assumed that if there was any news about Antonia's sisters, it would come from the Red Cross, so she was thunderstruck when one morning in the autumn of 1994, a letter for Antonia came with the rest of her morning post.

There was no clue as to who had sent it and Diana had only a vague idea where Byelorussia was, but she ran down the street as fast as she could, clutching the envelope, and burst into Antonia's house.

'It's for you,' she gasped. 'It came this morning.'

Antonia wiped the smear of marmalade off the

knife on her plate, and slit open the envelope. When she realized it was from her elder sister, Anya, she was quite literally struck dumb. She sat speechless in her chair until Diana could stand the suspense no longer and, as gently as she could, prised the letter from Antonia's fingers. She would have read it had it not been written in Polish.

'I don't understand,' Antonia said. 'It's from Anya, the big sister I told you about. But how . . .'

Diana explained that four years before she had asked the Red Cross to find out if Anya and the others were still alive.

'I would have told you it was impossible,' said Antonia. 'If you'd asked me.'

'I know. That's why we didn't tell you.'

'We?' Antonia drew the word out.

'I asked Mary and the others what they thought,' said Diana. 'Before I got in touch with the British Red Cross.'

'Remind me to have a word with my children,' Antonia said, but she was far too happy to be annoyed at being kept in the dark about what they had done.

She read the letter over and over again. Anya and her two sisters had been sent to Byelorussia after the war. They had never forgotten their sister but they assumed she had died in Germany. They were all still alive and lived quite close to each other. Antonia tried to cram the events of fifty-three years into the letter she wrote back. She talked about her dreadful time in Nazi Germany, her life in England, her children and grandchildren, and how happy she was to have heard from her sisters after so long, thanks to the Red Cross world-wide network.

The Search Continues . . .

At first, the Second World War didn't intrude too much on the British community in Burma. Things there continued very much as they had since the Victorians completed their colonization of the country in the late 1880s. Their lives mirrored the lives of their middle class relatives in the home counties: everything stopped for tea at four and everyone dressed for dinner! The continuous monsoon rains that fell from June through September were something that had to be tolerated, but the sheer beauty and riches of Burma were more than adequate compensation.

Things changed dramatically in 1942, when Japanese soldiers swept eastwards through Asia. As news came through that the Japanese had taken Hong Kong, Manilla and Singapore, panic-stricken colonials flocked to Rangoon, the capital, or Mandalay, the major city of Upper Burma, desperate to get on a boat or plane bound for India.

But they were little aware of what lay ahead for many of them – a nightmare trek along jungle tracks and through malarial swamps; over hills that from the distance glowed an inviting pale violet, but which close up loomed skywards, surely impassible to exhausted emigrants. A race against time, before the

162

monsoon turned fast-flowing rivers into raging torrents.

Among the refugees fleeing to safety was the Mellican family . . .

In the late nineteenth century, Donald Mellican's soldier grandfather and his grandmother sailed to Burma, where they settled down and brought up their family. When the First World War broke out, one of their sons, Arthur, enlisted in the army and was posted to the Middle East. The war over, Arthur returned to Burma where he married his sweetheart, Kathleen. Not long afterwards he was offered an engineering job in Moulmein on the Salween River across the Gulf of Martaban from Rangoon. Arthur and Kathleen raised their three sons and three daughters in this prosperous suburb set on a ridge dotted with large houses.

Their eldest son, Donald, was already a member of the Territorial Army when war broke out in Europe. He enlisted as an anti-aircraft gunner with the Royal Artillery and was sent to join his regiment in the north of the country.

Early in 1942, the Burmese received intelligence reports that the Japanese were massing in great numbers at Rahaeng (now Tak) just inside neighbouring Thailand. Knowing that it was only a matter of time before the invasion came, the British decided to destroy key installations in the city, hoping to make life difficult for the occupying troops. Arthur helped dismantle several of the projects he had helped build, knowing that when the Japanese attacked there was certain to be a price on his head.

In the early hours of 20 January 1942, the advance guard of the 56th Japanese Division crossed the border into Burma. By this time Arthur, Kathleen and their five other children had arranged flights out of Rangoon and had already left for the city. Arthur's brother, John decided to stay put. He was among the first to be arrested by the Japanese, who mistook him for his brother. John died shortly after, while in custody – his family remains convinced he was executed.

Meanwhile, the Mellicans had arrived in the capital to find it had already been taken by the Japanese. They were sent to an airstrip on the outskirts of the city, only to find it had been bombed, as had the next . . . and the next . . . and the next, travelling farther and farther north each time. Eventually, they arrived in Myitkyina on the banks of the Irrawaddy – Japanese bombers had already destroyed the air strip there. There was only one escape route open to them; the Mellican family and hundreds of others stranded in the town would have to walk through the Hukawng Valley into Assam in India.

The country in that area is some of the harshest in the world, difficult enough in the dry season, almost impassible during the monsoon when torrential rains turn jungle tracks into quagmires. No one knows how many died on the trek of disease, hunger and exhaustion. One survivor recalled his horror at watching twenty men, women and children embark on a bamboo raft to cross the river, only to be swept to their deaths.

Meanwhile, Donald's battalion had been losing its ongoing battle against the advancing Japanese army. He had no way of knowing what had happened to his family. His only momento of them were snapshots which he kept carefully hidden between the support strut and tarpaulin of his truck. After some particularly intense action, the battalion was ordered to use the last of their heavy ammunition in one final bombardment, before destroying the cumbersome artillery and then trying to walk through the jungle to India, carrying what small arms and light guns they could. Donald never saw the photographs of his family again.

However, he was one of the lucky ones; he made it safely to India, but almost as soon as he arrived there, he came down with malaria. When he recovered, he was given twenty-eight days' leave which he spent at the Loretto Convent in Calcutta, where refugees who had trekked from Burma were arriving daily. Donald scanned every group as it arrived in case his family was among them; he described them to everyone he met, but no one had seen them. When his leave was over, he left a message on the convent notice board, asking for anyone who had news of Arthur and Kathleen Mellican or their children to contact him c/o his regiment.

A few months later, he received a brief note from a woman he had known in Burma, which contained the devastating news that his parents, three sisters and one of his brothers were all dead. His mother had succumbed to exhaustion and malnutrition a few days into the trek. A few days later his brother Pat had died of septicaemia after a small cut had become a festering wound. The three girls died shortly afterwards. The woman went on to write that she had heard, but couldn't be sure, that before he died Arthur had chanced upon a group of Gurkhas who had agreed to take the only child still living, eight-year-old Reg, with them.

Donald survived the war and returned to Burma as an instructor with the Burmese Army. Just before the country became independent in 1948, Donald and his wife, Dorothy, an old friend from pre-war days in Burma whom he had met again in Assam, sailed for Britain. They lived for a while in Manchester, before moving to Maidstone when Donald entered the prison service.

Donald loved his wife and doted on their four children, but he never forgot his parents, brothers and sisters, and often wondered what had happened to Reginald. Had he made it to India with the Gurkhas? Had he died of exhaustion, malaria or malnutrition in the jungle? Or had he been killed in an ambush? He promised himself that one day he would try to find out exactly what had happened to his little brother, but it took a heart attack in 1973 to make him realise time was running out. Forced to take early retirement, Donald now had time for his quest.

The first thing he did was to write to the Indian, Pakistani and Bangladeshi High Commissions and the Burmese Embassy in London – none were able to help. Donald perservered. One evening when he was watching *This Is Your Life* on television, he had an idea. If the researchers could reunite the 'star' of the show with relatives from the other side of the world, perhaps they could at least give him some advice on what he could do to find Reg. The producer was sympathetic, but was unable to help.

He contacted the Salvation Army, who were equally sympathetic but explained that they too could not help in this particular case. When he got in touch with the British Red Cross, he was disappointed to learn that, as Japan had not been a signatory to the Geneva Convention, it had no obligation to give the ICRC the names of soldiers or civilians taken prisoner or who had been identified as having died in Japanese controlled territory. They explained that they would need more details before further steps could be taken.

Donald set about writing to every official organisation he could think of, asking if there was any reference to a Reginald Mellican in their files. And then, in 1983, some time after he had written to the British Library, an official there replied that the name Mellican appeared in a record it had compiled of Europeans who had fled Burma in 1942. A Miss Vardun had reported the deaths of Mr and Mrs A Mellican and their four children between Shinbwinyang and Tipong.

Four children! So Reg must have gone off with the Gurkhas. Perhaps he *had* survived after all. Donald went back to the Red Cross and told them what he had found out.

The Red Cross in London agreed do what they could to help. While there was no direct evidence that Donald's brother was still alive, there was nothing definite to suggest that he had died. Over the next three years they sent out their tracing enquiries to a wide variety of sources. Sadly, Reg's whereabouts, if he is alive, are still unknown, but the case remains open. Donald is in touch with the British Red Cross. New information recently found in the ICRC archives is even now being followed up, and may yet establish if Reginald

167

Reunited!

Mellican survived the long trek from Burma to Assam.

Donald continues to hope that Reg made it to safety and was perhaps sent to an orphanage, or was possibly adopted. If so, and if he is still alive, he would be just into his sixties.

If anyone who reads this book knows a man called Reginald Mellican who believes all his family died in Burma, or who knows what happened to him, his brother and the British Red Cross in London would dearly love to hear from them.

A Man of Action

In 1978, Dr Omar Dihoud arrived in Britain from Somalia, for urgent treatment to restore his failing sight. He was opposed to the regime that held power in Mogadishu, and while he was in London he was instrumental in setting up the anti-government Somali National Movement (SNM), an activity that made it impossible for him to return to Somalia. Therefore, he applied for political asylum in the United Kingdom.

Until 1988, the SNM had made forays into Somalia from inside Ethiopia. When the Ethiopian government told them to abandon their camps, SNM troops launched a full-scale offensive into the north-west of their homeland. The response from Mogadishu was as lethal as it was swift. The bombs and artillery shells that landed on the SNM stronghold towns of Hargeisa and Burao, killed thousands of innocent people and sent hundreds of thousands of others fleeing into Ethiopia.

Omar was safe in London but his thoughts were with his family in Hargeisa, especially Farah, his frail, elderly mother. When he asked the British Red Cross for help in finding out if she had survived the bombs, he was given a standard tracing form which was duly sent to the Central Tracing Agency in Geneva.

Geneva wrote back that, because of the volatile situation in the area, the ICRC had no presence in northern Somalia and was unable to undertake any tracing enquiries. Omar was reassured that the information he had supplied about his mother had been recorded and, as soon as the situation eased, every effort would be made to find her.

In the meantime, they asked the British Red Cross to arrange for Omar to complete a tracing form that had been specially revised to help them cope with the mounting number of tracing enquiries for missing Somalis. The CTA knew that, if they were given the green light to start work in the country, to be successful they would have to get to grips with the intricate network of tribes, clans and sub-clans which form the base of Somali social structure. Omar was asked to supply the names of any friends or family who may still be in Hargeisa, so that when work began, Red Cross workers would know which clan elders to approach for help.

They were also aware that Somali culture is very much an oral rather than a written one, so they weren't too surprised when the first news that Omar had of his family came in the form of a tape cassette sent by a friend in Djibouti. Omar was relieved to hear that Farah and other members of his family were thought to have made it to the safety of the Ethiopian refugee camps. But he was horrified when he heard that his niece, Faisa, had been badly injured by a land mine.

Omar's anxiety intensified as the months passed and there was no more news. And then, in February 1990, he heard from the British Red Cross that Red Cross workers in Ethiopia had made contact with his mother, who was very sick, and ten of her grand-children in a camp in one of the most barren areas of the country.

Omar's anxiety about his mother turned to desperation when he read the plea for help scribbled on her behalf on a Red Cross Message. He had to get his family out of the camp and bring them to Britain.

The British Red Cross advised him to seek the assistance of the United Nations High Commission for Refugees (UNHCR) in London. At the same time, the ICRC referred the case to the UNHCR in Ethiopia. Both organizations gave full backing to Omar's request that his family be brought to London on humanitarian grounds and be granted political asylum there. But Omar was just one among hundreds of Somalis who were trying to get their families into Britain – all on humanitarian grounds.

Frustrated by the prospect of endless delay and desperate for news of his mother, Omar decided to take matters into his own hands and managed to find the money to fly to Ethiopia to see her.

The flight from London to Addis Ababa takes about twelve hours. The hazardous journey from the capital to the refugee camp is bumpy and dusty and takes twice as long. When Omar eventually found his mother, he knew as soon as he saw her that he had to do whatever it took to get her to Britain.

The first thing he did when he got back to London was to contact the Home Office. When staff there told him that it could take another six months before they reached a decision, he turned to the British Red Cross for help.

Staff there were horrified when they heard what Omar had to tell them. One of his sisters had already died of hepatitis and another had been killed in a bombing raid on Hargeisa. One of his brothers had also been killed and another had gone missing: Omar suspected he was being held by the authorities in Hargeisa. His nephews and nieces only had their grandmother to look after them and she had been so weakened by malnutrition and diarrhoea that she had been unable to rise from the rags that were her sick bed to greet her son.

'I got there just in time,' he said. 'They would all be dead by now if I hadn't been able to buy them food and medicine.

'You can't begin to comprehend the conditions there,' he went on. 'People have no money to buy what food there is. There's no sugar, no cooking oil, no kerosene.

'All around is a wilderness: a hot, windy, lifeless wilderness. There are no relief workers, no schools for the children, there are no drugs, not even an aspirin. People just sit around waiting to die.

'I don't want my mother and family to die. I am their only hope. They must live.'

As soon as Omar had left, a Red Cross tracing officer telephoned the Home Office to ask if once again someone could check on the progress of Omar's application for family reunion.

The very next day he was told by the British Red Cross that Farah and her grandchildren had been granted political asylum in Britain. The news had already been telexed to the British Embassy in Addis.

Omar had been concentrating on his first hurdle but two more remained. How was he going to get his family from this remote area to Addis, and who was going to pay all the travel costs to the UK? Some countries have special funds for such cases: Britain is not one of them.

Omar approached the UNHCR for help but their funds were already stretched to the limits. The ICRC helped to get Farah and her grandchildren to Addis, but there were no funds available that could be used as a contribution towards their airfares from Ethiopia to Britain. Omar borrowed as much as he could from friends and contacts and scraped together enough money to pay for their tickets.

He was overjoyed when he was reunited with his family in London, but he was not the sort of man to let matters rest there. Omar Dihoud was well aware that many Somalis in London were suffering from the trauma of the war and the psychological effects of not knowing if their families were alive or dead; and if alive, whether they were still in Somalia or in an Ethiopian refugee camp. So he set up a counselling service to help his community cope with the stress many were experiencing.

When north-west Somalia became more peaceful in 1991, Omar was able to return to Hargeisa where he established a psychiatric referral centre. Nearly two thousand Somalis, most of them young, many of them stricken with post-traumatic stress disorder, have already been seen.

Somalia has many troubled days ahead. Luckily, there are many others like Omar who will continue to strive to establish services in their country. But sadly, peace remains an elusive ideal in many parts of the country and families remain separated; waiting for the day when they can once more be together.

A Rwandan Reunion

In 1994 another name was added to Biafra, Vietnam, Cambodia, Bosnia and the other horrors of the twentieth century where the Red Cross has been active in its more than 130-year history: Rwanda.

Since 1993 United Nations troops had tried to prevent Rwanda's suicide. But following the death of their president in a plane crash in 1994, the Tutsis and Hutus turned on each other with a ferocity that horrified the watching world. The terror that was unleashed in the ensuing civil war was unlike anything Africa has experienced in its long, turbulent history.

The ICRC had been working in Rwanda with local staff for almost two years. Many of the Red Cross delegates in Rwanda were all too aware of the truth of the horrific stories about roads paved with bodies and rivers clogged with corpses.

At least half-a-million Rwandans were massacred during the turmoil and four times that number left the country and fled into Tanzania, Burundi and Zaire. Among them were two little Tutsi boys, five-year-old Evode and his brother Alexander who was seven.

They had been in church with their mother, Emilia, and her neighbour, a Hutu woman called Freda. Emilia and Freda were old friends. While they hoed their fields and gathered sweet potatoes, their children played together, oblivious to the fact that they were from different ethnic groups.

Suddenly the calm inside the church was shattered by the sound of gunfire, and a few moments later Hutu soldiers burst into the church, guns ablaze. With bullets ricocheting off the corrugated-iron roof, Emilia pushed Evode and Alexander into Freda's arms. 'Look after them,' she begged, knowing full well what lay in store if they were spotted by the troops. 'Promise you'll get them out of here and look after them.'

Freda promised and put her arms around the two boys. And when the soldiers ordered the Hutus outside they didn't give Evode and Alexander a second glance as they left the church, their faces buried in Freda's skirts.

As she and the children ran home, Freda could only imagine what was happening in the church. The Tutsi men would probably have been shot right away and their defenceless women repeatedly raped before they, too, were gunned down or hacked to death.

When they were safely home, Freda told the two terrified boys that their mother had asked her to take them away from the village with her own children.

'Where are we going?' asked Evode. 'Is Mummy coming with us?'

'Away from here. Away from the fighting,' said Freda, ignoring the second question.

'Is Mummy coming with us?' persisted Alexander.

'Not now. She'll join us later, when she can,' said Freda.

She waited until first light the next day, before she led Evode, Alexander and her own three children out of the village and headed for Tanzania. A car could have made the journey in a few hours, but it took the bedraggled group several days to reach safety along the tracks. More than once they had to hide in the undergrowth when the rumble of trucks told them that soldiers were on the move.

At first, they were on their own, but as they trudged along under the relentless sun, they met up with more and more men, women and children fleeing from the barbaric civil war. By the time Freda and the children, weak from hunger and thirst, crossed into Tanzania at Rusumo Falls they realized that they were a tiny part of a mass exodus of terrified refugees. They eventually reached a vast refugee camp that had sprung up a few miles over the border at Benaco. The camp was the temporary home of three hundred thousand Rwandans, mostly Hutus. There was little shelter and hardly anything to eat for the hungry children who queued at the food distribution centres for a handful of grain. But at least there were no machine guns and no machettes; at least the refugees were alive.

The longer she was in the Hutu camp, the more concerned Freda became for Emilia's children, should it be discovered they were Tutsi. She became so scared for them that when she heard there was a Red Cross orphanage in the camp, she decided that was the best place for them. When she got there, she told a nurse everything that had happened and begged her to take Evode and Alexander in.

'But what about you?' the nurse asked anxiously.

'I have my own children to look after. We're quite safe,' she said. Then she turned to Evode and Alexander, told them to be good boys and made her way back to her hut. No one knows if she is still alive.

The little that Freda had told the nurse at the orphanage about Evode and Alexander was sent to the ICRC Tracing Service in Nairobi, where an ambitious registration programme was already under way. The aim of the project was to collate details of all unaccompanied Rwandan children under the age of sixteen who had been taken into care by the Red Cross, and eventually to try to trace a surviving relative willing to care for them.

Similar schemes had been undertaken before, but the scale of the Rwandan crisis dwarfed even the largest of them. By the end of 1994, forty-eight thousand children had been registered. By the time it is complete, this figure will probably have more than doubled.

There was so much to be done that the ICRC asked National Societies to send experienced tracing personnel to help, which is how Pam Hussain found herself in the sultry heat of a Tanzanian refugee camp, thousands of miles away from Grosvenor Crescent in London, talking through an interpreter to Evode and Alexander, who were surprisingly unscathed by their experiences.

'What do you think happened to your mother?' Pam asked them very gently. 'Do you know where she is?'

'Soldiers came to the church,' said Evode. 'We think they killed her.'

Pam was astonished at how calm Evode was.

'And your father?'

'We don't know where he is.' It was Alexander

who answered this question, again, Pam noted, with amazing calmness.

'Do you have any uncles or aunties?' Pam asked.

'Only Auntie Win!' said Alexander.

'Do you know where she lives?' Pam didn't really expect a seven-year-old to know his aunt's address, but to her surprise Alexander gave her Win's full name and her address, in a village not far from his own.

The situation in Rwanda was still too volatile for any attempt to be made for the two boys to go and live with their aunt, so it was decided that they should stay at the Benaco orphanage for the time being.

A few days after Pam had talked to the boys, a man turned up at the orphanage, saying he was a relative and claiming that their father had asked him to find his sons and take them back to Rwanda. But when some of the things he said failed to tally with what Evode and Alexander had told Pam, the Red Cross refused to let them go. A few days later, another person came to the orphanage, again saying he was from the boys' father. It was obvious that Freda had been right, Evode and Alexander were in danger; so they were sent to a Tutsi camp about four hours journey from Benaco.

The information about the two brothers had been put on the computer data base and Patrick Amin, an ICRC delegate, crossed the border to try to contact the boys' Auntie Win. The address that Alexander had given Pam Hussain was not quite accurate, but it was close enough to make the task of finding Win and telling her that her nephews were still alive quite easy.

'Were they right? About their mother being killed?' Patrick asked.

'Yes. No one got out of the church after the Hutus were told to leave.'

'So Evode and Alexander are orphans?'

Win frowned. 'I don't think so,' she said after a moment or two. 'Their father went to Kigali months ago, before the trouble started. I think he's still there.'

Once Patrick had arranged with Win that she would look after the two boys when it was safe for them to return, he left her house to walk back to his Jeep. He had no sooner clambered aboard and switched on the engine, when he heard a voice shout, 'Mr Patrick! Mr Patrick!' He glanced in his mirror and saw Win running towards him waving her arms wildly in the air.

'Mr Patrick,' she panted. 'Can you find my Luke? My eldest boy. He left the village weeks ago and I haven't heard from him since. Can you find him for me?'

Patrick wrote down all that Win could tell him about her son and promised to do everything he could to trace him. Sadly, when he got back to Tanzania, he found out that Luke had been killed. He asked a witness to write a Red Cross Message to Win giving her the news, which was delivered by a priest who lived near her.

A few months later, when the fragile peace that had been established between the Tutsis and the Hutus looked as if it was going to hold, Pam Hussain was asked if she would escort Alexander and Evode across the border and take them to Win's house.

By this time the boys had settled into their new

home and had made so many friends with the other children that they were a little reluctant to leave. Their foster-mother helped Pam to settle Alexander and his brother into the back of the Red Cross Jeep. Then she stood on the steps in the middle of a group of children, all waving goodbye until it was out of sight.

As they crossed into Rwanda, Alexander nudged Evode in the ribs and cried, 'Look, Evode. Kagera!' the name of the river which runs along the border between Rwanda and Tanzania – to the children proof they were really going home, to Pam and the rest of the world, the river that had been choked with dead bodies.

As they drove further into Rwanda, the boys began to recognise local landmarks and were soon jumping up and down with excitement. When Pam brought the Red Cross Jeep to a halt outside Win's house, the boys' aunt and her children came running out to meet them. There were whoops of joy as the cousins skipped around the Jeep and helped Evode and Alexander down, inundating them with questions.

'What happened to you?'

'Where have you been?'

'What have you been doing?'

When the clamour had died down, Alexander reached for Pam's hand and squeezed it, saying, 'We went with the neighbour and then the Red Cross took care of us.'

Alexander and Evode are now living with their father.

The Years Ahead

The stories recounted in this book reveal all too clearly the dreadful consequences of armed conflict on families, which affect not just those directly involved but also future generations. In 1992, the plight of an anxious Bosnian father, who had contacted the British Red Cross to find his two sons, highlighted the effects of current conflicts on families and was a warning of needs for the Tracing and Message Services in the future.

Rwanda, Somalia, Afghanistan and the former Yugoslavia are just some of the countries whose conflicts over recent years have caused millions of people to flee their homes, some displaced within their own country but many seeking refuge in other countries. Luckily for this Bosnian man, thanks to British Red Cross records, when his request was entered into the computer it was matched instantly with the name of one of his sons who wished to send him a Red Cross Message from Scotland. Contact was quickly restored. Sadly, for many others, such comforting news is not to be received so quickly and the consequences of these population movements will be of a long duration, and certainly well into the next millenium.

While efforts to find lasting and effective solutions to these conflicts continue, the International Red

Cross Movement continues to strive to minimize the human cost of separation on families. Red Cross family Tracing and Message Services are as important today as at any time in the past in restoring and maintaining contact between separated family members. They provide a vital link which can help ensure that, when peace returns, people can try as quickly as possible to start their lives together again.

The activities of tracing delegates of the ICRC today in registering and compiling information on victims of war will help families to be in touch for many years hence. The staff and volunteers of the British Red Cross, working with other Red Cross and Red Crescent Societies world-wide, continue to be a strong link in this unique and humanitarian chain.